*Expert Advice for Women Who Have or
Are Starting Their Own Business*

CAPITALIZING
ON BEING
WOMAN
OWNED

*Including Marketing Reasearch, Planning,
Government Support, and Tax Breaks*

JANET W. CHRISTY

CAREER
PRESS
Franklin Lakes, N.J.

CAPITALIZING ON BEING WOMEN OWNED
EDITED AND TYPESET BY KATE HENCHES
Cover design by Cheryl Finbow
Printed in the U.S.A. by Book-mart Press

To order this title, please call toll-free 1-800-CAREER-1 (NJ and Canada: 201-848-0310) to order using VISA or MasterCard, or for further information on books from Career Press.

The Career Press, Inc., 3 Tice Road, PO Box 687,
Franklin Lakes, NJ 07417
www.careerpress.com

Library of Congress Cataloging-in-Publication Data

Christy, Janet W., 1953-

Capitalize on being women owned : expert advice for women who have or are starting their own business including market research, planning, government support, and tax breaks / by Janet W. Christy.

p. cm.

Includes index.

ISBN-13: 978-156414-890-2

ISBN-10: 1-56414-890-4

1. New business enterprises—Management. 2. Women-owned business enterprises—Management. I. Title.

HD62.5.C46 2006

2006011948

ACKNOWLEDGMENTS

Thank you to Kristie Bohm who started me on this path when she asked me to help her "maximize [her] woman-owned business certification."

Thanks to Brenda Laakso who initiated the first form of this information when she asked me to develop and present a "Capitalizing On Being Woman Owned" workshop for the Greenville, South Carolina Chamber of Commerce.

Thanks to my two terrific daughters, Mandy and Megan, for believing that their mom can do anything.

And thanks especially to my husband, Mark, for providing support, editing, patience, and faith.

CONTENTS

INTRODUCTION

The good news is that this is probably the best time ever to be a woman-owned business. The bad news is that there are still no free lunches...or rides...or money!

The reason that this is such a good time to be a *woman-owned business* (WOB) is that there is a lot of attention focused on ensuring that WOBs have a fair chance at business opportunities. Government entities and businesses alike are setting and enforcing goals for the amount of money spent with WOBs. Federal, state, and local government agencies and institutions are establishing programs and centers dedicated to helping women and minority businesses get started and be successful. Groups for women business owners are being created all over the country to provide peer support, mentoring, networking, training, and technical assistance.

All of these things illustrate that the concentration is on helping woman/minority-owned businesses do business. The effort is to facilitate their entrance and success in the mainstream of business. This book is a guide to helping WOBs use the leverage of their woman-owned status in that business mainstream—to capitalize on being woman-owned. The majority of the guidance in this book is about marketing and selling because that is what will sustain your business and make it successful.

This book is not a guide to grants or free money for starting and running a business. If it were, it would be a guide to nowhere. I have done extensive research for clients, business centers, incubators, chambers, and government agencies to try to find grants for WOBs with miniscule success. The SBA (Small Business Administration) says it best on their Website (*www.sba.gov/expanding/grants.html*):

> *The U.S. Small Business Administration does not offer grants to start or expand small businesses, although it does offer a wide variety of loan programs. (See www.sba.gov/financing for more information.) While SBA does offer some grant programs, these are generally designed to expand and enhance organizations that provide small business management, technical, or financial assistance. These grants generally support non-profit organizations, intermediary lending institutions, and state and local governments.*

As the SBA says, they fund organizations that provide assistance to small businesses; some of their funds are specifically for entities and programs dedicated to woman-owned businesses. They provide funding to 110 different women's business centers throughout the country. Some of the centers are solely for women and some serve multiple types of small businesses. A list of the centers can be found by clicking on Women's Business Centers at *www.onlinewbc.gov*. Most of the centers are designed primarily for WOBs that are "financially challenged" and the programs reflect that; however, the services and resources are usually available to any woman and often open to the public in general.

Occasionally these centers will raise or receive funding that allows them to give small grants to WOBs, usually in the specific geographic area served by the center.

There are some grants available from certain federal agencies for the development of specific products or services, usually related to complex technology, homeland security, or bioscience. One of the programs specifically for small businesses (with some concentration on woman- and minority-owned businesses) is detailed at *www.sba.gov/sbir/indexwhatwedo.html*.

There are other federal government agencies and departments that provide funding in ways similar to the SBA—for centers or loan programs.

There are some tax breaks for small businesses that are available to woman-owned businesses. These breaks are credits, deferments, or incentives. They are normally provided to businesses because of job creation or because the business locates (or relocates) to an area that the local or state government is trying to develop, such as a poverty zone or downtown being redeveloped. Being woman- or minority-owned could be an advantage or criteria for receiving the tax relief, but ownership alone is not usually sufficient for qualifying.

This book does provide some guidance on finding assistance, training, information, and other resources. It is very important, though, to realize that most of the resources available are tools, not money, to help you establish and run your business. The money that is available is almost always in the form of loans.

As you use this book and other resources remember the old adage about teaching someone to plant a garden instead of giving them a meal. Another thought that will help you appreciate, or at least understand, the way things are done is that the government agencies, foundations, and supporters want to spread their funds to as many people and businesses as possible.

Capitalizing on being woman owned involves:

❏ making the most of it
❏ getting the most out of it
❏ benefiting from it
❏ profiting from it

The following pages will provide you guidance, assistance, and resources for doing these things as you start, build, and run your business.

Chapter 1

ADVANTAGES

There are many advantages to being a woman-owned business (WOB). Most of the current advantages are centered on business opportunities—finding them, capitalizing on them, and being prepared to live up to them.

There is a growing awareness of just how strong a presence woman-owned businesses have in this country. The number of WOBs is substantial and continues to grow at faster rates than any other types of ownership. The following are some statistics from the Center for Women's Business Research (*www.womensbusinessresearch.org*) that illustrate this:

- 10.6 million firms are at least 50-percent-owned by a woman or women
- 48 percent of all privately held firms are at least 50-percent-owned by a woman or women
- Between 1997 and 2004 the estimated growth rate in the number of Woman Owned Businesses was nearly twice that of the growth of all firms—17 percent for WOBs versus 9 percent overall

Because there is strength in numbers, woman-owned businesses are attracting more attention and therefore more business. Government entities at all levels, education institutions, and commercial businesses now realize that they can benefit from having a larger and more diverse vendor base. They also understand that they need to ensure WOBs get a fair share of the dollars they spend.

Here are some facts that translate as advantages for WOBs.

- ☐ The overall goal of the federal government is to award 5 percent of contract dollars to woman-owned businesses. Each agency sets its own specific goal, but it is at least 5 percent. These contracts may be direct between the federal government and the woman-owned business, or the woman-owned business may be a subcontractor to a prime contractor (the company that actually has the contract with the federal government).

- ☐ For contracts that are valued at $500,000 ($1,000,000 for public facility construction) a federal prime contractor must submit a subcontracting plan that includes a plan for the use of woman-owned businesses.

- ☐ Most states have a goal of at least 10 percent for the amount of procurement dollars they spend with minority-owned businesses. Some states set separate goals for woman-owned businesses.

- ☐ Many local government entities (cities, counties, and so on) have established goals for the use of woman- and minority-owned businesses. Those who have not set actual goals usually have programs and procedures to ensure that WOBs know about opportunities.

- ☐ Most state and local government entities require their prime contractors on construction projects to have subcontracting plans that demonstrate how they will use woman- and minority-owned businesses. Some require it on other major contracts, too. Some states even provide a tax credit to prime contractors that use woman/minority subcontractors.

❒ Education entities that receive government funding usually follow the lead of the entity that funds them.

❒ Most major corporations have both a formal program and goal to promote the use of woman- and minority-owned businesses within the company.

❒ Many major corporations have a policy that requires or at least encourages their Tier I suppliers to have a plan to use woman- and minority-owned businesses.

❒ Prime contractors to government need you.

There are other advantages that are indirectly related to business opportunities. Most of these have to do with the support and development of woman-owned businesses. These include:

❒ All federal agencies now have an Office of Small and Disadvantaged Business Utilization (OSDBU) to help the agency meet their diversity goals.

❒ Most states and many local government entities have personnel and even departments whose purpose is to aid woman- and minority-owned businesses in getting contracts.

❒ Most states and many local government entities use a certification process to screen out those businesses that are not truly woman or minority owned.

- ☐ Private organizations provide certifications that are recognized by commercial businesses to weed out businesses that are not woman owned.

- ☐ The United States Small Business Administration (SBA) has several programs to help woman-owned businesses successfully establish and run their businesses. These programs include training, counseling, online information, and loans.

- ☐ Numerous government entities, chambers of commerce and private organizations provide resources specifically designed to help women establish and run successful businesses.

- ☐ Some loan programs favor woman-owned businesses.

Philosophical advances that offer advantages and leverage to woman-owned businesses include:

- ☐ Organizations, centers, and programs focused on women in business are being created in amazing numbers.

- ☐ Businesses whose clients are predominantly business owners are developing marketing programs focused on women.

- ☐ Politicians along with federal, state, and community leaders are scrambling to find ways to address the needs and issues of woman-owned businesses.

- ☐ Women in business are helping each other.

Some philosophical negatives do exist, but identifying and understanding them can still provide you benefits and leverage. Some of these are:

- ☐ Because this has become such an attention-grabber agencies, organizations, and government/ education entities are looking for ways to "check" support and assistance for woman-owned businesses off their to-do lists.

Advantage: Help them to find something to check off that truly benefits you and other women business owners.

☐ Sometimes events held in the name of diversity are thinly disguised facades that have no substance, but make the hosts and sponsors feel noble.

Advantages: Attend because purchasers that need you will be there; participate in the planning and try to give the event some substance (the hosts and sponsors may simply be unaware that their event doesn't serve a real purpose).

☐ Some leaders think that once they have done something for women- and/or minority-owned businesses they are done. They do not understand that the goal is to level the field, not placate a special interest group.

Advantage: Take what they offer, but don't be embarrassed to ask for more now that you have their attention.

☐ Some non-woman-owned businesses resent the attention and assistance being received by WOBs.

Advantage: Offer to partner with them so they can take advantage of the opportunities and resources.

☐ You feel shameful when you use your WOB status. You're afraid you won't be recognized for your abilities and competence.

Advantage: The current focus on WOBs is a wave, ride it while it lasts. You are not likely to get business solely because you are a woman-owned business; it has become more of a door opener and a differentiator or tiebreaker.

Chapter 2

APPROACH

My philosophy is that marketing is all about finding the right angle and using it properly. Woman-owned businesses have a built-in angle—the fact that it is *woman owned*. Learning how to leverage that angle is an important part of capitalizing on being woman owned.

Sometimes being woman owned is an advantage, sometimes it is an obstacle, and sometimes it is immaterial. You need to understand how to determine when to use the built-in angle and when another angle would be more effective.

In some cases a business, government, agency, or education institution needs or wants to use a woman-owned business to meet a goal, qualify for a contract, improve economic development, or simply help that business. Occasionally, a prospect will prefer to use a woman-owned business for a specific product or service because they feel a female enterprise is more capable, adds needed diversity, or is more comfortable. It is important to remember that there can be prejudices and preferences for WOBs as well as against them. The pages that follow explain the reasons for each of the categories—federal, state, and local government; and education and business.

This book is not about a fight for any cause. It is about understanding the current situation and climate for woman-owned businesses and working within that frame to have marketing success.

Research is vital to knowing when and how to use the angle of being woman owned. You must find out if the fact that you are woman owned is important to a business, government agency, or education institution. You have to do some investigating to determine if this angle opens a door or gives you an advantage. In the chapters to come, you will find information on how to conduct research and use the information gathered to develop a workable sales and marketing plan.

Note: In doing your research, you are looking for information on your prospect that guides you in marketing to them. In some situations you will find that being a woman-owned business is immaterial, but if your research is thorough it will provide you another marketing angle.

Key Words

When doing research to find prospects, there are some key words and phrases that will help you. Explanations are provided here. Chapter numbers where additional guidance concerning where and how to look for information are provided.

Goal—A business or government/education entity that has a supplier/vendor policy/plan often establishes percentage goals for the use of specific business classifications. These entities may establish an overall minority use goal or they may set goals by classification (that is, African American, Asian, Native American, woman-owned). Sometimes the goal will simply be for the use of small businesses, HUBs, or disadvantaged businesses. Woman-owned businesses either have their own classification or fit into one of the declared classifications. (See Chapters 4 to 10.)

HUB—Historically Underutilized Business. This is a classification used by some state government entities and companies to designate businesses that have been and may still be at a disadvantage in the business world because of the owner's race, gender, physical challenge, or location. This term is often used interchangeably with or instead of minority or disadvantaged. Sometimes HUB also includes businesses that are defined as small. (See Chapter 4 and 5.)

MBE—Minority business enterprise. In some situations this includes woman business enterprise. (See Chapters 4, 10, and 11.)

Minority—This term usually identifies a classification of business owner. It always includes race or ethnicity; it may or may not include women owners. (See Chapters 4 to 10.)

MOB—Minority-owned business. In some situations this includes woman-owned businesses. (See Chapters 4, 10, and 11.)

OSDBU—Office of Small Disadvantage Business Utilization. This acronym is primarily used by the federal government. All federal agencies have established a OSDBU to promote the utilization of small disadvantaged businesses by their respective agency. Variations of this term may be used by other government/education entities and by businesses. (See Chapter 4.)

Prime Contractor—This is the business that actually has the contract with the government agency or education institution. Normally referring to a business as a prime contractor means the business uses subcontractors in the delivery of the products or services of the contract. (See Chapters 4 to 10.)

Procurement/Purchasing—The process and/or department of a government agency, education institution, or business that is responsible and accountable for obtaining products and services. The people associated with this process and/or department are most commonly called purchaser, buyer, or procurement specialist. (See Chapters 4 to 10.)

SDB—Small Disadvantage Business. This is primarily used by the federal government to identify a business that meets stringent requirements. The business must be judged by the Small Business Administration (SBA) to be disadvantaged. A few other government/education entities or businesses may also use this term. (See Chapter 4, 10, and 11.)

Small Business Development Liaison—This is a position (or office) in a large business. The responsibility of this person (or office) is to identify responsible, capable small businesses for his/her company to purchase products and services from. The Liaison may also be charged with assisting in the actual development of the individual small businesses. Woman- and minority-owned businesses are normally included in this effort. In some companies, this position may be titled "Minority Business Development." A director or manager may be used in place of a liaison. (See Chapter 10.)

Supplier or Vendor Diversity—This is the term used to describe the philosophy of inclusion of all suppliers or vendors regardless of race, gender, size, or any other classification. (See Chapters 4 to 10.)

Supplier or Vendor Diversity Policy or Plan—These are the stated guidelines by a company, or government/education entity for the inclusion of all vendors. This policy or plan may also state goals for the amount of dollars spent with specific vendor classifications (that is, woman owned or minority owned). (See Chapters 4 to 10.)

WOB—Woman-owned business. (See Chapters 4, 10, and 11.)

WBE—Woman business enterprise. (See Chapters 4 to 10.)

Commitment of Prospects

One piece of information that is important, whether you are researching government or commercial enterprises, is their "commitment level." You can determine the level of commitment by evaluating their policies, practices, reasons (for using woman-owned businesses), and history. You need to understand how to do this as demonstrated in the various sections on government and business.

Knowing the Prospect

Your research should include learning what the business or government/education entity does and how they do it. Many will provide a list of products and services they purchase, but this is just a starting point. If you understand what the business, agency, or school does and gain some idea of how they do it, you will better position your company to:

- Know if you provide a product or service that is applicable but not on their published list.
- Identify the reasons why being woman owned gives you an advantage.

- ☐ Determine where and how to publicize/advertise your business to reach your prospects.
- ☐ Differentiate yourself.
- ☐ Prioritize your prospect list.

If you do not do this research you will likely waste your marketing time and money. It does not work to just "throw" the information out there and hope the right people see it. This book will provide you detailed information, by prospect type, on where and how to conduct this research.

In doing research for my individual clients, one of the most common complaints I find is that businesses did not bother to find out anything about their prospects. As one representative of a large international corporation put it, "How can they expect to sell me something if they don't know anything about my company?"

The research should be integrated into all your marketing activities, including:

- ☐ Development of an overall marketing plan
- ☐ Development of marketing materials
- ☐ Prospecting strategy
- ☐ Advertising plan
- ☐ Contact to individual prospects

When you are ready to contact a prospect you should ensure the information you have is *no more* than three months old. If you are recontacting a prospect or customer/client you want to be sure the information you have on them is still current and applicable.

You will differentiate yourself and use your prospecting time more efficiently if you take the time to do the research before you contact a potential or current customer/client. This not only shows that your prospect or customer/client is important, it also saves them time because dealing with you requires less explanation from them.

Chapter 3

FIRST STEPS

In order to make your marketing research, planning, and actions effective you need to make some choices that will help focus your time and effort. In doing research for small business development organizations I have been told by trainers, bankers, and entrepreneurial developers that one of the primary reasons businesses fail is that they do not identify their prospects. As one banker put it, "They have a skill or desire and want to build a business around that skill or desire. But too often they don't know who will buy their service or product. If they do know who their customers will be, they don't know anything about them or their buying criteria. I don't know how they can expect to succeed."

Focusing your research will allow you to identify and get to know your potential clients or customers. Making choices about territory, prospects, and products/services will maximize the time you spend in marketing research, planning, and activities.

Territory

You will need to choose a geographic territory. The world or even the country are much too large. You may one day cover these territories, but you need to break them down into workable pieces and determine the pieces on which to concentrate first. The specific geographic territory that is appropriate for your business depends on your products/service, your ability to reach that territory (travel, web presence, staff, cost of doing business, and so on), and other factors that make that area attractive and feasible.

Because the trend toward the use of woman- and minority-owned businesses is becoming widespread, this is probably not a major factor in choosing a territory. However, you may find, when doing research, that a geographic area does not have many businesses and government/education entities that have a supplier diversity policy/plan. In this case, you will either need to save that territory for a later date or use another marketing angle besides being woman owned.

Your appropriate territory may be your county, your state, surrounding states, or simply your city or town.

Once you have "worked" a territory, you will have more understanding of what makes an area appropriate and, therefore, which territory should be next.

Prospects

In order to make your research more efficient you need to narrow the list of prospects that you will investigate. Narrowing your list makes the research process less intimidating. Exactly how narrow you make your list is dependant on your business and also on the following factors:

❏ Time you (and/or your staff) have to spend on research

❏ Time you (and/or your staff) have to spend on marketing and sales activities once the research is done

❏ Your ability to deliver the products and services once you've made the sale

Do not attempt to bypass this step by using pre-prepared lists such as the inventory of local manufacturers, the chamber of commerce membership directory or a state government's Website list of agencies and institutions as your narrowed list. Also, do not use the membership roster of civic organizations and non-profit boards. The parameters of these lists have nothing to do with your business or the use of woman-owned businesses.

These are examples of rationale for narrowing a prospect list:

❏ Federal agencies that use your product or service (for example, Department of Housing and Urban Development (HUD)] if you do building renovation)

❏ Government agencies in your chosen geographic area (for example, state Department of Transportation (DOT), if you do grading or paving)

❏ Education Institutions in your chosen geographic area (for example, the local school district, if you provide educational software)

❏ Business types that are likely to use your product or service (for example, general contractors if you are an architect)

- ❑ Business types that you would like to sell your product and service to (for example, you provide employee screening to textile manufacturers and you know that you could provide the same type of service to automotive manufacturers)
- ❑ Specific businesses in your chosen geographic territory that use your product or service
- ❑ Specific businesses that are similar to your existing customers/clients (for example, you provide specialized printing services to several construction firms and want to expand to more construction firms in your chosen geographic territory)
- ❑ Prime federal or state contractors that use subcontractors (for example, you could provide advertising specialties to Public Relations firms that have contracts with federal agencies)
- ❑ The suppliers of your prospective and existing customers/clients (*Note: many large corporations now expect, and sometimes even require, their suppliers to have vendor/supplier diversity plans.*)

Remember that you are narrowing the list of prospects on which you will do research to determine which ones use your products/services and can benefit from the fact that you are woman owned. At this point, you cannot narrow your list according to their level of commitment to using woman-owned businesses unless you already have knowledge that their commitment level is high. You are primarily trying to establish a starting point for your research. This list of prospects will be coordinated with your chosen geographic territory.

Product/Service Focus

The third choice that you must make before starting your research is to decide which of your products and/or services will be your focus. Of course, if you only offer one product or service, this choice is simple. However, if you can provide several products and/or services you may need to choose one or two for the initial research.

Not limiting the number of products or services that you use in your research will result in one or more of the following:

- ❑ A list of prospects that is so long you never tackle it
- ❑ All your time spent on research
- ❑ Contacts that are a waste of time
- ❑ Lots of initial contacts and no follow up; therefore few customers/clients gained

In my research for clients and workshops, purchasers tell me that very often a vendor/supplier offers too many choices. This can be confusing to a prospect. It can also make them wonder if your business is too fragmented and therefore cause doubt about your ability to deliver or perform. Purchasers in business, government, and education are all looking for vendors/suppliers that can do the job. Focusing your research on prospects for a few of your products and services and then basing your marketing efforts on that research, will help you present a more professional image to your prospects. It will also give you a reason for recontacting them in the future—to tell them about another product or service.

As with your chosen territory and prospect list, the focus on the products and services that you use in your research can be shifted or expanded in the future.

Chapter 4

Identifying and Qualifying Prospects:
FEDERAL GOVERNMENT

The commitment level of the federal government and its agencies to use small, minority- and woman-owned businesses has increased dramatically over the last few years. The overall goal of the federal government is to award 5 percent of contract dollars to woman-owned businesses. Each agency sets its own specific goal. These contracts may be direct between the federal government and the woman-owned business or the woman-owned business may be a subcontractor to a prime contractor (the company that actually has the contract with the federal government).

In this chapter we will explore ways and places to identify and qualify federal government prospects.

Initial Step

An essential first step for doing business with the federal government, either direct or as a subcontractor, is to register with the CCR (Central Contractor Registration) *www.ccr.gov*.

CCR is the database used by the federal government and its prime contractors to identify potential vendors/suppliers.

All businesses must register on CCR to be considered for contracts with the federal government or its prime contractors.

Data is collected, validated, stored, and distributed by CCR to agencies of the federal government. The information is also available to prime contractors looking for subcontractors.

It is very important that the CCR registration is completed accurately because the information is shared with federal agencies and is used for electronic payment. It is also important that the information be kept up to date. Inaccurate information may rob you of opportunities. Some common inaccuracies are:

☐ Typographical errors (that is, transposed letters or digits, letters left out)

☐ Incomplete address or e-mail address

☐ Missing or incorrect identification codes (that is, North American Industry Classification System [NAICS]—the leading coding system used to identify business types, the Website to determine your NAICS is *www.naics.com*)

☐ Outdated information (that is, old address, phone number, contact name)

Direct Selling

All federal government agencies are potential prospects. However, all are not valid prospects. As stated in earlier chapters, it is vital to do research in order to find the best prospects. You must determine which federal agencies need your specific products and/or services and have a high commitment to the use of woman-owned businesses.

I don't recommend that you start researching with the *A*s and work your way down the whole list of federal agencies. You can make some logical assumptions about which federal agencies are likely to use your products and services. This will help you prioritize your list for research. You can find a good list of federal agencies with links to their procurement/purchasing information on the SBA (Small Business Association) "Buying Sources" Web page at *www.sba.gov/businessop/findop/buying.html.* Once you have decided on the likely users of your products/ services then you can look at the procurement/purchasing information and determine which ones are valid prospects.

To decide which agencies to contact try to match your products/services to the function of the agency, for example:

- ☐ If your business is an agricultural one then consider the Department of Agriculture and the Department of the Interior.
- ☐ If you provide healthcare services consider the Department of Health and Human Services.
- ☐ If you offer drug screening/testing consider the Department of Justice.
- ☐ If you manufacture or sell security equipment consider the Department of Homeland Security and the various military branches.

All federal agencies now have an OSDBU (Office of Small and Disadvantaged Business Utilization). The OSDBUs are charged with helping their agency meet its diversity goals. Federal agencies encourage you to contact them so they can help you determine if your products/services are a good match to the needs of a specific agency. You can find links to all OSDBUs at *www.osdbu.gov.*

Another good source of information on specifically what an agency buys and uses is the FedBizOpps Website (*www.fedbizopps.gov*). This Website is where all federal agencies post their procurement opportunities with a value of more than $25,000. The Website is a good source of immediate opportunities on which you may be able to bid. It is also the best information about what each agency is spending money on and which agencies use your specific products or services. If you are not sure if an agency is a valid prospect it is a good idea to look at this Website even before you spend your time contacting that agency's OSDBU. Most of the procurement/ purchasing information websites for federal agencies will refer you to FedBizOpps. This Website is set up so you can search for opportunities by federal agency in the following ways:

- ☐ Sub agency, office, department
- ☐ Location
- ☐ Posted date—date the opportunity was posted to FedBizOpps
- ☐ Product classification—product or service type
- ☐ NAICS (North American Industry Classification System)—industry type
- ☐ Set aside—contracts that are designated to be awarded to a specific business type such as:
  - ▪ Small disadvantaged business
  - ▪ Woman-owned business
  - ▪ Minority-owned business
  - ▪ Veteran-owned business
  - ▪ Very small business
- ☐ Awards—contracts that have been awarded recently

Investigating the Set Aside and NAICS portions of the various agencies on the FedBizOpps Website will help you determine if that agency is a prospect for your specific products or services. This is especially helpful if you are not sure which Agencies are a good match for your business. It will also provide you with information that you can use in tailoring your marketing message to that specific agency; how to use that information is covered in Chapter 12 of this book.

The information in the Set Aside and Awards sections of FedBizOpps are indicators of the level of commitment or trend to the use of woman-owned businesses (or other category that may include woman-owned) for that particular agency. It is very common for an agency to only use the "Total Small Business" classification for all their Set Asides instead of breaking the opportunities out into the individual classifications previously listed. Agencies post solicitations, revisions, and new information to FedBizOpps as needed, so you need to look at the site frequently.

Because it does take time and persistence to look at the FedBizOpps Website often enough to take advantage of the opportunities that apply to you, they have provided an alert service. You can actually sign up to receive bid opportunities/ solicitations that are appropriate for you. There is no guarantee, though, that you will receive notifications on all opportunities that apply to the product/service classifications you choose, so you should still check the Website often.

Tip: Almost every Website or other posting of specific opportunities is an excellent source of information on trends and issues. Use this information in qualifying and prioritizing your prospects.

Assistance for Direct Selling

SBA (Small Business Administration) is the federal government's primary resource for all types of small businesses. One of its major functions is to help small businesses be successful at selling their products and services to federal Agencies. The SBA Website (*www.sba.gov*) provides information on several topics that are valuable in identifying and qualifying prospects. These include:

- How the Government Buys (*www.sba.gov/ businessop/basics/buys.html*)
- Online Women's Business Center (*www.onlinewbc.gov*)

- ☐ Federal Acquisition Regulations (*www.sba.gov/businessop/rules/far.html*)
- ☐ Online training (*www.sba.gov/training/courses.html#MARKETING%20&%20ADVERTISING*)
- ☐ Classes and workshops by region (*www.sba.gov/calendar*)
- ☐ Library (*www.sba.gov/training/library.html*)
- ☐ Matchmaking events and services (*www.businessmatchmaking.com*)

The SBA has district offices that administer the agency's programs and provide more localized information and assistance. Information on all the district offices can be found at: *www.sba.gov/aboutsba/dis_offices.html*. The district offices sponsor opportunities to meet face to face with procurement/purchasing representatives of federal agencies in trade fairs and matchmaking events. Usually these events include "how to" information sessions with specific federal agencies. These events are great opportunities to identify and qualify prospects.

The SBA also provides funding to other organizations that can provide resources and information. Information on three of these other organizations follows:

SBDCs (Small Business Development Centers)—These centers are a partnership between SBA and state/local government and education institutions. In addition to providing training, management counseling and technical assistance, the centers also provide one-on-one assistance on government procurement. They will provide trends, contact information, and guidance. Links to all 1,100 SBDCs can be found at *www.sba.gov/sbdc/sbdcnear.html*.

WBCs (Women's Business Centers)—There are more than 80 WBCs throughout the United States that receive funding from SBA. The centers are usually tailored to meet the needs of the specific area they serve. Many of them are good resources for information that will assist you in identifying and qualifying prospects. A complete list of the centers is provided at *www.onlinewbc.gov/wbc.pdf*.

Some of the centers sponsor conferences that include opportunities for woman-owned businesses to meet one-on-one with government agencies, education institutions, and large corporations who are committed to Supplier/Vendor Diversity.

SCORE (Service Corps of Retired Executives)—This is a volunteer organization that conducts training and provides individual counseling for all types of small businesses. Some of the retired executives worked for federal agencies or for federal prime contractors. They can provide insight into the buying trends that will help you in your identification and qualification efforts. You can find information about the SCORE office closest to you at *www.score.org*.

Another good Website for procurement forecasts and other qualifying information is *www.womenbiz.gov*. This Website is a gateway for woman-owned businesses that want to sell to the federal government. It is sponsored by the National Women's Business Council, which is a federal advisory council that, as an independent source, provides advice and policy recommendations to SBA, congress, and the president on issues that are important to woman-owned businesses. Forecasts for federal agencies can be linked to from *www.womenbiz.gov/forecasts.html*. This site also provides a list of WOBREP (Woman Owned Business Representatives) for most federal agencies on this Web page: *www.womenbiz.gov/advocates.html*.

Many federal agencies provide detailed information on their Websites about the products and services they purchase. The Websites often include information about their policies, philosophies, projections, and goals. Some of those Web pages are listed below:

- ☐ Bureau of Alcohol, Tobacco, and Firearms (ATF) *www.atf.gov/acquisition/index.htm*
- ☐ U.S. Department of Justice
  www.usdoj.gov/jmd/osdbu
- ☐ U.S. Department of Agriculture
  www.usda.gov/da/smallbus/frame3.htm
- ☐ U.S. Department of Commerce
  www.osec.doc.gov/osdbu/Selling_to_DOC.htm
- ☐ U.S. Department of Labor
  www.dol.gov/osbp/regs/procurement.htm
- ☐ U.S. Department of the Interior
  http://ideasec.nbc.gov/forecast
- ☐ U.S. Department of Transportation
  *http://osdbu.dot.gov/osdbu_services/
  Procurement/forecast.cfm*
- ☐ U.S. Environmental Protection Agency
  *http://yosemite.epa.gov/oarm/oam/
  forecastdatabase.nsf*
- ☐ U.S. Department of Health & Human Services
  www.dhhs.gov/osdbu/publications/forecast.html

Some federal agencies are committed to using woman-owned businesses, but have found it difficult to reach the goals they have set. Therefore they have developed special programs or committees to try and increase the amount of business they award to woman-owned businesses. Two examples of this are:

- ❑ U.S. Department of Transportation
  http://osdbu.dot.gov/osdbu_services/
  Women_Services.cfm.
- ❑ U.S. Department of Defense
  www.acq.osd.mil/osbp/doing_bisiness/index.htm

Note: Women business owners often think that their chances of getting contracts with government agencies perceived as male dominated are very slim. However, the fact that the departments of transportation and defense have established committees to increase the number of woman-owned contractors shows that the chances are not slim at all. In doing research for my clients and workshops, buyers for several military bases have told me that they are constantly looking for more woman-owned businesses.

A good Website for identifying procurement opportunities and resources for small businesses is *www.Business.gov*. This site is a partnership between SBA and several other Federal Agencies. The opportunities are listed on: *www.business.gov/topics/government_contracting/procurement_opportunities/index.html*. This information is much like FedBizOpps because it provides immediate opportunities and helps you identify agencies that use your products/services.

Knowing where to find information that will help you identify and qualify federal government direct prospects is only half of the process. Developing a list of specifications to use when doing research will assist you in gathering and analyzing the information you find. A suggested general process is provided in the following chart.

Process for Gathering and Analyzing Information on Federal Government Prospects

Question	Next Step	Tips/Notes
Does the federal agency have need of my products/ services?	If yes move on to the next question. If no remove agency from your list.	
Does the federal agency have a specified goal for the amount of money to spend with woman-owned businesses?	If yes move on to the next question. If no move agency to the bottom of your list.	If you know the agency has immediate need of your products/services, then consider approaching them using a different angle than woman-owned. For instance, use the fact that you are a small business because they are required to have a goal for small business even if they do not break it down into subcatagories.
Does the federal agency have need for my products/services in my specified geographic area(s)?	If you cannot find this information, then skip to the next question.	FedBizOpps, forecasts for federal agencies and the agency's OSDBU are good sources for this information.
Does the federal agency have a location/site/office in my specified geographic area(s)?	If yes, move on to the next question. If no, move agency down your list for reconsideration when your specified geographic area includes the locations/sites/offices of this agency.	The agency's Website and local telephone directories are two good sources for this information.

Question	Next Step	Tips/Notes
Does the federal agency have a designated WOBREP (woman-owned busness representative)?	Make note, this is an important qualifying and prioritizing fact.	
Does the federal agency have any set asides for woman-owned businesses?	Make note, this is an important qualifying and prioritizing fact.	If the answer is no, analyze the agency's amount of set asides for other categories such as very small business and small disadvantage business.
Does the federal agency have a history of awarding contracts to woman-owned businesses?	Make note, this is an important qualifying and prioritizing fact.	The awards section of FedBizOpps is one of the best places for this information; so is the agency's Website.
What is this federal agency's philosophy for using woman-owned businesses?	Make note, this is important qualifying and prioritizing information. If they do not have a policy specific to WOBs, look at the overall philosphy for use of small and minority businesses	The agency may have a published policy or plan. This will provide some information, but should not be your only input. You should also talk with other sources such the Agency's OSDBU, it's WOBREP, the SBA, and the local SBDC.

Question	Next Step	Tips/Notes
Are opportunities with this federal agency more likely direct between my company and the agency or are they more likely subcontracting opportunities?	If the opportunities are more likely direct then move to the next question. If the opportunities are more likely subcontracting then skip to the analysis process for subcontracting.	Identifying and qualifying subcontracting opportunities are covered in the second part of this chapter.
After gathering information on 10 to 20 agencies, sub agencies, locations, sites, and offices, analyze and rank them according to the previous questions. Do not limit yourself to one federal agency (such as the Department of Education) but diversify your research the first few times so that you increase your opportunities.	This should be your first list of prospects to contact for selling direct. Once you have made initial contact to each of these you will be in the next phase of marketing with them. At that point you should restart the identification and qualification process with new potential prospects.	Remember that in an effective marketing plan you will always have several prospects in each phase. We are only covering the initial phase in this chapter.

Subcontracting

Sometimes the best way to market to the federal government is through subcontracting. This means that your company provides a portion of the products and/or services specified in a contract. That contract is actually between the federal government and a prime contractor. Your contract would be with the prime contractor.

Some of the reasons why this approach may be advantageous for you are:

☐ You might not be equipped or qualified to handle the project alone.

☐ You may not want to attempt the project alone or as the prime contractor because:
- the project is too complex.
- the project is too time consuming.
- requirements for such things as insurance or bonding are financial obstacles
- it is a Set Aside for another category of HUB (Historically Underutilized Business) such as minority- or veteran-owned and you can partner with a qualifying HUB with them as the prime contractor.

☐ The project covers multiple geographic areas and you cannot serve all of them.

It is important to remember that a federal agency can meet its goal for using woman-owned businesses (and for small businesses as a whole) through direct contracts *or* subcontracts. Sometimes it is more efficient for them to use a large company as the prime contractor. However, in these cases they normally require that the prime contractor use HUBs as subcontractors. For contracts that are valued at $500,000 ($1,000,000 for public facility construction), the prime contractor must submit a subcontracting plan that states specific goals for the use of each category of HUB. These plans must include a description of the efforts used to ensure that HUBs have an equal opportunity to compete for subcontracting opportunities. These plans are reviewed before a contract is awarded and reports must be submitted at specified intervals. There are penalties for the prime contractor if it fails to comply.

Because a company bidding on a project may not be awarded the contract unless they have a small business subcontracting plan and because they may be penalized if they do not follow their plan, they are looking for qualified, responsible subcontractors.

There are several Websites and resources for identifying and qualifying prime contractors and subcontracting opportunities. Some of these are discussed in the following paragraphs.

SUB-Net is the premier Website for listing and identifying subcontracting opportunities. It is also an excellent place to find prime contractors who definantly use subcontractors. The Website is sponsored by SBA (Small Business Administration). It allows prime contractors to post solicitations for subcontractors and it allows potential subcontractors to search for opportunities. The site is at times used by federal agencies, state and local governments, nonprofit organizations, colleges/universities, and other small businesses to find providers of specific products and/or services. So, it is a good source of information for identifying and qualifying all types of prospects. The SUB-Net Web address is *http://web.sba.gov/subnet/index.cfm*.

On SUB-Net you can search for opportunities by:

❐ NAICS (North American Industry Classification System)—industry type.

❐ Description—key words.

❐ Subcontract Solicitation (if you know that the solicitation exists and you have the number).

❏ Place of Performance. (*Tip: Very often prime con-tractors will post solicitations for specific products/ services in multiple locations.*)

SBA provides a list of prime contractors located in each state that offer subcontracting opportunities. The prime contractor is listed by the state in which they are headquartered; however, they may need subcontractors in other states, depending on the requirements of their contract(s) with the federal government. Contact information is provided. The Website is *www.sba.gov/GC/indexcontacts-sbsd.html.*

Several federal agencies have, through their OSDBUs (Office of Small Disadvantaged Business Utilization), published lists of prime contractors seeking subcontractors. Some examples are provided in the following paragraphs. These are supplied primarily as examples to aid you in research for your own specific prospects.

USDA (U.S. Department of Agriculture)

Purchasing and contracting for the USDA is very decentralized. The agency has more than 200 field procurement offices; however, most of the large procurements that require a subcontracting plan by the prime contractor are handled at the headquarters or at the 11 major contracting agencies. The USDA's annual Procurement Forecast and a Small Business Subcontracting Directory can be found on the agency's Website at *www.usda.gov/da/smallbus/sbonline1.htm*. This directory lists existing prime contractors and provides contact information and the specific products and services that they need from subcontractors.

USDOJ (U.S. Department of Justice)

This federal agency includes several bureaus and offices:
❏ Prisons
❏ DEA (Drug Enforcement Administration)

- ❑ FBI
- ❑ Federal Prison Industries
- ❑ Immigration and Naturalization
- ❑ Justice Management
- ❑ Office of Justice Programs
- ❑ U.S. Marshals

The list of prime contractors seeking subcontractors for each of these is found at *www.usdoj.gov/jmd/osdbu/ prmdir00.htm.*

USDOL (U.S. Department of Labor)

There are 18 sub agencies within the DOL. The list of prime contractors for each is on the Website *www.apps.dol.gov/contract_grant/report_inter.asp.*

USDOI (U.S. Department of the Interior)

The Website listing the prime contractors is *www.doi.gov/ osdbu/primecon.htm.*

The Interior's procurement authority is decentralized and rests with individual bureaus and offices. There are 13 bureaus and offices.

USDOT (U.S. Department of Transportation)

The prime contractor list for this agency can be found at *http://osdbu.dot.gov/osdbu_services/procurement/ subcontracting_directory.cfm.*

USEPA (U.S. Environmental Protection Agency)

This agency lists all of its contractors, whatever their size or type. The list can be found at *http://cfpub.epa.gov/sbvps/*

search.cfm. They also list all existing contracts at *www.epa.gov/ osdbu/contracts.htm*. Analysis of these two lists can provide information on subcontracting opportunities.

USDOD (U.S. Department of Defense)

The prime contractor list for the Department of Defense can be found at *www.acq.osd.mil/sadbu/publications/subdir/ index.html*. The Pentagon is in the process of a $1 billion renovation; this project offers another universe of subcontracting opportunities. The project Website is *http://renovation. pentagon.mil/businessopps.htm*.

U.S. Department of Health and Human Services

The Top 100 prime contractors for this agency are found on this Website:

www.dhhs.gov/osdbu/read/primecont.html.

One of the best ways to find potential prime contractor prospects is by researching the actual *Contract Awards*. Even though there may not be an opportunity for you in the project for which the contract has been awarded, there could be future opportunities with the prime contractor that received the award. Some of the sources for award information are:

❐ FedBizOpps (*www.fedbizopps.gov*).

❐ Agency Websites.

❐ Existing prime contractor Websites.

The table on page 46 provides a suggested process to determine if prime contractors are viable prospects.

Process for Gathering and Analyzing Information on Federal Government Subcontracting Prospects

Question	Next Step	Tips/Notes
Does the business have a contract or is it bidding on a project that requires a subcontracting plan?	If yes, move on to the next question; if no, move the business to the bottom of your list.	Most agencies list existing contracts or provide that information through their OSDBU. FedBizOpps also lists contract Awards.
Is the prime contractor working or bidding on projects for which my products/services are appropriate?	If yes, move on to the next question. If no, remove prime contractor from your list.	
Does the prime contractor have a contract or is bidding on a project that needs my products/services in a geographic area I can serve?	If yes move on to the next question. If no, reevaluate prime contractor in the future for match of geographic area.	
Does the prime contractor already have their subcontracting plan?	If no, contact immediately. If yes, move on to the next question.	The prime contractor and the agency OSDBU are the best sources for this info.
If there are no opportunities on a current contract, is it likely the prime contractor will bid on future projects for which my products or services and geographic area are appropriate?	If no, move to the bottom of your list for future contact. If yes, move on to the next question.	OSDBU, FedBizOpps and the prime contractors Website (customer/client info) are good sources.

Question	Next Step	Tips/Notes
Does the prime contractor have a history of subcontracting with woman-owned businesses?	If yes, move on to the next question. If no, try to determine why and decide whether or not to pursue.	Remember that this book is about capitalizing on being woman-owned, not fighting causes. If convenience or something similar is the reason there is no history of using woman-owned businesses this may still be a valid prospect.

The following questions are designed to help you evaluate the potential prospect and do not necessarily build on each other.

Question	Next Step	Tips/Notes
Is the federal agency involved in the project or bid struggling to meet their goal for the use of woman-owned businesses?	Enhances your chances.	The agency's Website or OSDBU will provide this information.
Are there other qualified woman-owned businesses listed on CCR (Central Contractor Registration) that provide the appropriate products/services in the designated geographic area(s)?	If not, your chances increase.	Remember that a business must be listed on CCR in order to be used as a subcontractor.

Question	Next Step	Tips/Notes
Does the prime contractor have a designated diversity contact (small business liaison, minority bus-developer, and so on) or is the listed contact more general in nature (purchaser, project manager, etc.)	This does not necessarily increase or decrease your chances, but it does provide you some insight for your dealings with the prospect.	The title of the contact is normally provided on the prime contractor list.
After gathering information on 8 to 10 prime contractors analyze and rank them according to the previous questions.	This should be your first list of prospects to contact for subcontracting. Once you have made initial contact to each of these you will be in the next phase of marketing with them. At that point you should begin the identification and qualification process over with new potential prospects.	Remember that in an effective marketing plan you will always have several prospects in each phase. We are only covering the initial phase in this chapter.

Chapter 5

Identifying and Qualifying Prospects:
STATE GOVERNMENT

Just as the federal government has increased efforts to be inclusive and supportive of woman-owned businesses, so have most states.

In order to maximize your prospecting and marketing time, it is critical to first identify and qualify the states that have a strong commitment to the use and support of woman-owned businesses. The purpose of this chapter is to aid you in identifying and qualifying those states. It is not feasible to provide lists or specific information because the philosophies and actions of the states are constantly changing. Some of the general reasons for this are:

- ☐ Change of elected or appointed officials (governor, head of Department of Commerce, head of Department of Revenue, Secretary of State, and so on)
- ☐ Change in laws (Procurement Code, incentives, and so on)
- ☐ Receipt of federal grants
- ☐ Opening or relocation of new business or industry that strongly supports woman-owned businesses (or at least minority-owned businesses)

In the following pages you will find information that will assist you in determining which states provide you with the best opportunities for capitalizing on the fact that you are a woman-owned business.

Where to Begin

I suggest that you begin your research with your home state. The research will be easier because of familiarity and your access to people who can help you. Once you have determined if your home state is a legitimate prospect, you will have a better understanding and can use that to conduct more efficient research in other states.

After researching your home state, it is best to have a plan for expanding your exploration into other states so that you build on your efforts and findings. There are several approaches you can use to conduct research on additional states:

- Research bordering states, widening the circle until you have researched all the states that you can physically and logically serve.

- Conduct research in states where you have additional presence such as an office, plant, or sales person.

- Conduct research in states where you have existing customers/clients.

- Conduct research in states that have similarities to your home state that are relative to your product or service, such as this scenario: states that use the same online training software and have a similar delivery method as your home state and your sale-related equipment.

State Policy and Philosophy

The first step is to determine if the state has a published policy for the use of woman-owned businesses. Most states do have a policy and it is for the use and support of minority-owned businesses (MOB) or minority business enterprises (MBE). Most states include non-minority women business-owners in the minority classification. However, do not take for granted that all states recognize non-minority women as a minority in the business world. Some states have programs specifically for woman-owned businesses, but do not include them in "use" goals set for state agencies, departments, and institutions. A state may use other terms in their policy such as: *Historically Underutilized Businesses* (HUB) or disadvantaged businesses. The policy will normally include such things as:

- ❐ Who qualifies as a minority (or HUB or disad-vantaged business)
- ❐ How qualifying businesses will be identified (that is, a certification process, self-declaration, and so on)
- ❐ Why there is a policy
- ❐ Acknowledgment that minority businesses have historically been restricted from or hampered in participation in free enterprise
- ❐ How the state will support and facilitate minority business participation in government procure-ment and free enterprise
- ❐ Goals for the use of minority businesses by state agencies, departments, and institutions and by prime contractors
- ❐ Incentives for the use of minority businesses

Even though the agencies, departments, and institutions of all 50 states may be eventual prospects for your business, some states have a culture and situation that will be more favorable to you than others. There is a guide later in this chapter on page 61 to help you determine the best states for you.

It is important to keep in mind that even the most strongly stated policy is only as good as the people who implement it.

When researching state governments as prospects, it is essential to also learn about the philosophy. The philosophy has to do with the attitude and approach. If the policy was established years ago by the state legislature, but the state employees do not feel a commitment to carrying out the policy, then the scenario is not the best one for capitalizing on being a woman-owned business. This is not the only evaluation criteria for determining the best state prospects for you, but it is an important one. The philosophy is not usually stated or published but can be seen in the following:

- [ ] Establishment and support of an agency/office/department to assist and promote the use of minority-owned businesses (If the state has an agency/office/department dedicated to the use and support of woman-owned businesses that makes a state an even better prospect)

- [ ] Reporting requirements for the use of minority businesses

- [ ] Rewards for state agencies/offices/departments for the use of minority businesses

- [ ] Requirement of prime contractors for the use of minority businesses on state projects

- [ ] Incentives for the use of minority businesses by prime contractors (that is, tax credits)

- [ ] Activities that promote the use of minority businesses (that is, trade fairs, matchmaking events, training, and so on)

- [ ] Accountability by state agencies, departments, institutions, and prime contractors to use minority businesses

Most states have a separate department that handles road and bridge construction and repair. The name for this department is the Department of Transportation and is commonly referred to by its acronym: DOT. This department very often has the strongest program for the use of woman- and minority-owned businesses as prime contractors and subcontractors. The department also usually does its own certification and has the most stringent qualifications. The reason for the high level of opportunities and the strict certification requirements is that this department must meet federal guidelines because much of their money comes from the federal government. More information on the certification is provided in the Chapter 11.

Policy Implementation

The policy of any entity (government, education, business) is only as effective as the implementation. When you are doing your research you cannot assume you have found a good prospect just because they have a policy and the policy uses the appropriate words. You must determine how the process and people make that policy a reality. This section provides some guidance on taking your research beyond the policy and philosophy.

Most states establish some type of office or department to implement the policy for the use and support of minority businesses. That office or department normally falls under the direction of the governor's office or the Department of Commerce. Depending on the philosophy of the state, the office/department will be aligned with economic development or procurement (the purchasing arm of state government). Some states have an office/department for the development and support of small businesses in general that may include a separate initiative for woman and/or minority businesses.

The office/department normally has a name that includes one or more of the following:

- ❏ Minority business
- ❏ Small business

- ☐ Underutilized business
- ☐ Assistance
- ☐ Utilization
- ☐ Support

When doing research on a state start your hunt for this office/department by using the previously mentioned terms through the state's Website search engine. If that is not successful or the state's Website does not have a search engine, look at the governor's Web page. The next possibility is the Procurement or Purchasing Office or Department. The third possibility is the Department of Commerce. If you cannot find that they have an office or department on the Website here are some other ways you can find out:

- ☐ Ask the governor's office
- ☐ Ask the Procurement/Purchasing Department/Office
- ☐ Ask the regional SBA (Small Business Administration) office or SBDC (Small Business Development Center)

This office/department is the embodiment of the state's philosophy. When doing research to identify, qualify, and prioritize state's for prospecting, it is crucial to become familiar with this entity including but not limited to its:

- ☐ Reputation (have they won any awards, what do minority businesses say about it)
- ☐ Adequately staffed (this is a measure of the value the state places on this effort)
- ☐ Actions and activities (such as networking and matchmaking events, newsletters, and development workshops)
- ☐ Attitude (what is said and does it match what is done, is it in the helping or telling mode)
- ☐ Areas of concentration (does it focus on a particular segment of the minority business community)

- ☐ Awareness of current situations and trends (are its efforts in harmony with the realities)
- ☐ Acceptance and acknowledgement by other state agencies, departments, and institutions (is it considered a help, a hindrance, or invisible)
- ☐ Inclusiveness of woman-owned businesses
- ☐ Efforts to promote the use of woman-owned businesses (or at least minority-owned businesses) by state agencies, departments, institutions, and prime contractors

Most states require that woman and minority businesses be certified in order to qualify for assistance or use by the state and its prime contractors in meeting the set goals. The office/department that implements the state's policy normally is responsible for certifying the woman, minority, and/or small businesses. Certifications are covered in Chapter 11.

The office/department that is responsible for the minority business program normally holds state agencies, departments, institutions, and prime contractors accountable if accountability is part of the policy and/or philosophy. If the office/department publishes reports on the use of minority-owned businesses, this shows the level of accountability by the state. The report provides information on which agencies, departments, institutions, and prime contractors do and do not use minority-owned businesses. Sometimes the reports will be broken down by category such as non-minority-woman-owned, minority-woman-owned, minority-male-owned, veteran-owned, and so on.

Direct Selling

To determine the best prospective states for your business you need to have some understanding of the procurement/purchasing process to find the opportunities and the buying trends. The following information is designed to help you gain that understanding and find the opportunities, both immediate and long term.

Although each state has its own set of rules, there are some commonalities. The basic ones include:

- ☐ The rules are law and are established by the state legislature.
- ☐ All agencies, departments, and institutions must follow the rules precisely.
- ☐ There is usually a "rules administration" office/ department. Some common words in the names for this office/department are:
  - ■ Procurement
  - ■ Materials Management
  - ■ Purchasing
  - ■ Vendor
  - ■ Business Opportunity
  - ■ Budget
- ☐ All opportunities over a specific dollar threshold (set by each state, but typically any solicitation valued at $10,000 or more) will be posted on the state Website.
- ☐ States normally post contract awards (winning bidder) on their Websites; they will often provide notification of the contract award to those who bid. You can also request the contract award information because it is public information.
- ☐ There is a vendor registration process (usually online is preferred) that allows potential vendors to place on record specific information about their business and its products or services for viewing by purchasing representatives of state agencies, departments, and institutions.

❐ Many state agencies, departments, and institutions have their own purchasing or procurement person or staff, however, they still must follow the rules.

You will want to spend some time exploring specific Websites and information in order to determine if a state is a good prospect for you. The following information will help you decide if proposing and providing services/products are feasible and cost effective for you and, in turn, will assist you in determining which agencies, departments, and institutions are good prospects. Here are some examples of areas you will want to explore and the information/understanding you will gain:

❐ The purchasing/procurement Website will likely provide:

■ Staff contact information and the guidelines for interacting with them (that is, "You must submit all questions by e-mail")

■ Definitions of responsibility (that is, IT purchases are made by the Office of Information Technology, not the Procurement Office)

■ Levels and rules of competition (that is, procurements more than $25,000 must be done by sealed bid)

■ Preferences (that is, a preference of X percent is given to state resident vendors over non-state resident vendors)

■ Evaluation guidelines

■ Payment terms

■ Incentives and tax credits

❐ Contract examples or the purchasing/procurement Website will provide standard contract requirements and language. This is vital in determining if you can meet the requirements and if you can afford the expense of meeting the requirements. The contract sections will likely include such things as:

- Insurance
- Indemnification
- Bond requirements
- Legal requirements such as: Force Majure, Save Harmless, Default, and Termination

☐ Websites that post the opportunities—Invitation for Bids, Request for Proposals, and so on—provide information on the current needs and buying trends of a state. Access to most of these sites is free, but some states do charge a small annual subscription fee to cover the cost. (These sites will also provide you with immediate opportunities.)

☐ Websites that post the contract award notifications provide information on buying trends, amounts spent for goods and services (clues to budgets), and the state's prime contractors (more information on prime contractors is covered on page 63).

☐ The Website of the office/department responsible for woman/minority business development and support sometimes provides helpful information. The Website supplies clues and indicators to help you identify and qualify your prospects. This Website usually includes such information as:

- Agencies, departments, and institutions that are seeking minority vendors

- Specific minority-supplied products and services needed
- Special programs, events, and opportunities
- Reports on the goals and the actual dollars spent by state agencies, departments, and institutions with woman/minority-owned businesses
- Changes in policies, goals, programs, and so on.
- Awards and recognition of agencies, departments, and institutions for use or support of woman/minority vendors
- Training

- The governor's Website will tell you what he/she thinks is important—importance translates to where the state will spend its money.
- The Website of the state legislature will allow you to see what bills are passed; again this indicates where money will be spent.
- The specific Websites of each agency, department, and institution furnish procurement/ purchasing information such as:
  - Staff
  - Policies
  - Opportunities
  - Important issues and trends

Other entities whose Websites can provide information on issues key to state expenditure trends and priorities include:

- State Chamber of Commerce—normally provides updates on legislation and trends that affect business
- Organizations associated with state governments such as:

- Association of Procurement/Purchasing Officers (the official name varies)—these are the people with the state and its agencies, department, and institutions that make the purchases. Their conferences and workshops are excellent sources of trend information and often provide opportunities for you to exhibit and sell your products/services.
- Association of Budget/Finance Officers (this does not exist in all states)
- Specialized groups such as, IT, homeland security, health and human services, economic development, and so on.

❑ Economic Development organizations can include information on:

- Programs for small, woman, and minority businesses
- Business recruiting and development efforts
- Announcements of new and expanding businesses (not only trending information, but also potential commercial targets)
- Indication of the state's philosophy about woman- and minority-owned businesses

A suggested general process for conducting research to identify valid state government targets for your business is provided in the following pages.

Process for Gathering and Analyzing Information in State Government Prospects

Question	*Next Step*	*Tips/Notes*
Does the state have a published policy on the use and support of women-owned businesses?	If yes, move on to the next question. If no, but they have a goal for use of minority-owned businesses that includes woman-owned businesses—continue on to the next step. If the state does not have any goals for minority-owned business use, consider a different approach if you wish to try to do business with this state.	
Does the state have a specified goal for the amount of money to spend with woman-owned businesses?	If yes, move on to the next question. If no, but they have a goal for use of minority-owned businesses that includes woman-owned businesses—continue on to the next step.	If the state does not have any goals for minority-owned business use, consider a different approach if you wish to try to do business with this state.
Does any state agency, department or institution have current projects related to your products/services?	If yes, move on to the next step. If no, research further to determine the buying trends and plans.	Use the information in this section to research the Websites of the state agencies, departments, and institutions.

Question	Next Step	Tips/Notes
Does any state agency, department, or institution have need of my products/ services in a geographic area you can serve?	If yes, move on to the next question. If no, move the agency lower on your list for reconsideration when your service area and the state's needs are a better match.	Use the information in this section to research the websites of the state agencies, departments, and institutions.
Do the identified state agencies, departments, and institutions have a designated person to work with woman-owned businesses (or minority businesses, or even small businesses?)	Make note, this is an important qualifying and prioritizing fact.	Use the information in this section to research the Websites of the state agencies, departments, and institutions.
Do the identified state agencies, departments, and institutions have a history of awarding contracts to woman-owned businesses?	Make note, this is an important qualifying and prioritizing fact.	Use the information in this section to research the Websites of the state agencies, departments, and institutions.
Are opportunities with these identified agencies, departments, and institutions more likely direct with my company or are they more likely subcontracting opportunities?	If the opportunities are more likely direct, move to the next question. If the opportunities are more likely subcontracting then skip to the analysis process for subcontracting.	Identifying and qualifying subcontracting opportunities are covered in the second part of this chapter. (Page 63.)

Question	Next Step	Tips/Notes
After gathering information on five to 10 agencies, departments, and institutions within a valid target state, analyze and rank them according to the previous questions. Do not limit yourself to one state but diversify your research the first few times so that you increase your opportunities. If you are only interested in one state increase the number of agencies, departments, and institutions.	This should be your first list of prospects to contact for selling direct. Once you have made initial contact to each of these, you will be in the next phase of marketing with them. At that point you should restart the identification and qualification process with new potential prospects within a state. At the same time you should be looking at additional states so you can begin the process of identifying specific agencies, departments, or institutions.	Remember that in an effective marketing plan you will always have several prospects in each phase. We are only covering the initial phase in this chapter. (Marketing strategy is covered in Chapter 12.)

Subcontracting

There are actually two potential targets to identify and qualify—the state itself and the prime contractors of that state.

States and their agencies, departments, and institutions engage in contracts with businesses that are referred to as the prime contractor. Most states have some type of program/effort to promote the use of woman and minority-owned businesses as subcontractors by prime contractors. (The subcontractor is considered a representative of the prime contractor.)

Many states also promote the use of other groups as subcontractors; these groups may include small businesses, veteran-owned, and Disadvantaged Business Enterprise (DBE).

Some of the ways that states promote the use of minority subcontractors (including women) are:

- Encouragement or requirement of goals for the use of minority subcontractors
- Contract requirement condition that prime contractors use or make a "good faith effort" to use minority subcontractors. In the last few years, many states have established guidelines and measurements for what constitutes a "good faith effort." The prime contractor is usually required to do one or both of the following:
  - Submit a utilization or subcontracting plan
  - Show proof of contracts or attempts to obtain minority subcontractors
- State income tax credit of X percent of the contract between the prime contractor and the subcontractor.
- Some states post subcontracting opportunities on the procurement/purchasing or minority program Websites.
- Some states only have minority subcontractor programs for construction projects; but usually these programs are strong and the requirements of prime contractors are strictly enforced.

If a state does not have some type of program to promote the use of minority subcontractors then, no matter what their policy or philosophy, that state's program cannot be as strong as the one that does.

Once you have determined that a state is a good target for your business, you want to move on to identify prime contractors and determine which ones are true prospects.

Information on the prime contractors can be found in the following places:

❑ Existing contracts with a state (often called state-wide contracts, term contracts, multiple award/vendor contracts, or simply "contracts"). These contracts are usually listed by type of product or service so you can quickly find the prime contractors who are real prospects for you.

❑ Posting of Contract Awards, which are usually on the Procurement/Purchasing Websites. The notice of award will provide a general label of the product or service (that is, laptop computers, janitorial service, or temporary staffing) and the name and contact information of the prime contractor. However, the notice of award does not usually provide any details or specifics. The best method for identifying projects for which you may be a subcontractor candidate is to follow the trail in this manner:

■ Monitor the postings of opportunities and identify those for which you can provide a portion of the products or services.

■ Watch the awards Website to see which vendor actually gets the contract.

■ Even if there is not an opportunity for you to subcontract on this specific contract, you have identified a business that qualifies as a prime contractor.

❏ Go through at least part of the process of bidding or submitting a proposal. This will provide
you an opportunity to find out what businesses
are interested in the opportunity. One or more
of these may present a subcontracting opportunity for you. There are steps within the bidding/
proposal process that offer a chance to identify a
potential prime contractor:

■ Sometimes the process requires a
"statement of intent to bid" so that
addendums to the original request for
bid/proposal can be sent. Sometimes
the addendums will include a list of
potential bidders/proposers.

■ For larger projects there is usually a
pre-bid meeting/conference. This is
an excellent opportunity to actually
see prospective prime contractors. It
is worth attending these meetings; even
if you do not intend to bid/propose,
it is still an excellent opportunity for
identification and qualification of subcontracting prospects.

■ A request for a bid/proposal may allow vendors to submit questions. You
should participate in this even if you
do not intend to propose because this
will allow you to see the questions
(usually identified by vendor) and the
answers. This is great information to
use in your identification and qualifying efforts—a vendor may expose its
subcontracting needs in the questions
it asks.

❑ Newspaper announcements about contract awards

You may have to do additional research to qualify the prime contractors you have identified. Just because they provide products or services that are related to yours, does not mean they are true prospects. They may have a situation that causes them not to be a good prospect. Some of the possible negatives that may cause a vender not to qualitfy are:

❑ They may be able to do everything themselves.

❑ They already have a partnership/subcontracting arrangement with another company. (This does not mean you should cross them completely off your list, they may be a prospect later.)

❑ They may have a subsidiary or sister company that does what you do.

❑ They may have a bad reputation for the way they treat subcontractors (be sure you find out the whole story before you cross them off your list).

❑ They may not really be qualified to bid/propose.

The following table provides a suggested process to determine if prime contractors are viable prospects.

Process for Gathering and Analyzing Information on State Government Subcontracting Prospects

Question	Next Step	Tips/Notes
Guide for Finding Prime Contractors With Existing Contracts		
Does the state have existing contracts that involve my products/services?	If yes, move on to the next question.	There are tips in this chapter on page 65 about where and how to find the existing contracts.

Question	Next Step	Tips/Notes
Who is the prime contractor on the existing contract that involves my products/services?	Move on to the next question.	
Is this prime contractor capable of meeting all contract requirements alone?	If yes, move to the bottom of your list. If no, move on to the next question.	
Does this prime contractor already have a subcontractor that provides the same products/services as you?	If yes, still consider contacting the prime contractor, but understand that this is a long-term possibility. If you do contact them, find out how strong the relationship and contract with the current subcontractor is. If no, move on to next step.	
Will this prime contractor benefit from using a woman-owned business (or minority-owned business if that classification includes women)?	If no, consider a different marketing angle to use if you want to pursue being a subcontractor to this prime contractor. If yes, contact them.	This chapter covers possible benefits.

Question	Next Step	Tips/Notes
Is there a bidding or RFP opportunity that involves my products/services?	If yes, move on to the next question.	Tips on finding opportunities are covered in this chapter on page 58.
Is there a way to find out who the potential bidders or proposing vendors are?	If yes, move on to the next question.	Tips on obtaining this information is provided in this chapter on pages 65-67.
Are the bidders or proposing vendors capable of meeting all the contract/project requirements?	If no, move on to the next question. If yes, move them to the bottom of your list and consider contacting them for future subcontracting opportunities.	
Does this prime contractor already have a subcontractor that provides the same products/services as you?	If no, move on to the next question. If yes, still consider contacting the prime contractor, but understand that this is a long-term possibility. If you do contact them, find out how strong the relationship and contract with the current subcontractor is.	
Would the bidder or proposing vendor benefit from using a woman-owned business as a subcontractor?	If yes, they are a likely target for you. If no, consider contacting them using a marketing angle different from woman-owned.	This chapter covers possible benefits on page 64.

Question	Next Step	Tips/Notes
Are you familiar enough with the bidder or proposing vendor to know if they would be a good partner?	If yes, contact. If no, do additional research before contacting them.	Good sources for additional information include: the company's Website, the states existing contract list, and the pre-bid meeting.

The following questions are designed to help you evaluate the potential prospect and do not necessarily build on each other.

Question	Next Step	Tips/Notes
Does the prime contractor/bidder/ proposing vendor have a history of subcontracting with woman-owned businesses?	If yes, enhances your chances.	Remember that this book is about capitalizing on being woman owned, not fighting causes. If convenience or something similar is the reason there is no history of using woman-owned businesses this may still be a valid prospect.
Is the state agency, department, institution involved in the bidding/RFP project struggling to meet their goal for the use of woman-owned businesses?	If yes, enhances your chances.	The office/department responsible for implementing the state's minority business policy normally publishes reports showing the use of WOBs. Other advice on finding answers to this question is provided in this chapter on page 51.

Question	Next Step	Tips/Notes
Are there other qualified woman-owned businesses registered with the state able to provide the same products/services as you?	If not, your chances increase.	Remember that a business must be certified by the state (or other entity they accept) in order to meet the subcontracting requirements.
Does the prime contractor/bidder/proposing vendor have a designated diversity contact (small business liaison, minority bus developer, etc.) or is the listed contact more general in nature (purchaser, project manager, etc.)?	This does not necessarily increase or decrease your chances, but it does provide you some insight for your dealings with the prospect.	You will probably have to investigate the company to find this answer.

Note: You should be evaluating and contacting prospects for direct and subcontracting simultaneously. It often happens that when you are researching or prospecting for one track you find an opportunity in a different track.

Chapter 6

Identifying and Qualifying Prospects: LOCAL GOVERNMENT

The level of interest in and commitment to the support and use of woman-owned businesses by local governments varies greatly.

The first step in identifying and qualifying local government prospects is to understand what entities are considered local government. The typical local government entities are:

- ❏ Counties
- ❏ Municipalities (cities, towns)
- ❏ Public works
- ❏ Public utilities
- ❏ Law enforcement (police, sheriff)
- ❏ Fire departments
- ❏ Economic development organizations
- ❏ Airports
- ❏ Parks and recreation
- ❏ Special purpose districts
- ❏ Buildings, zoning, and planning
- ❏ Emergency services

- ☐ Local court system (Civil, Criminal, Probate, and Family)
- ☐ Library

To maximize your prospecting and marketing time and effort you should decide which local government entities are likely to use your products or services. Then you can begin to identify and qualify the ones that have a strong commitment to the use and support of woman-owned businesses. This chapter will help in the identification and qualification of those local government entities. As with states, the philosophies and actions of local government entities that affect their level of support and commitment constantly vary because:

- ☐ Change of elected or appointed officials (Council, Board, Director, Manager, and so on)
- ☐ Change in laws (Procurement Code, incentives, and so on)
- ☐ Receipt of grants
- ☐ Opening or relocation of new business or industry that strongly supports Woman Owned Businesses (or at least minority-owned businesses)

This chapter provides information and direction to assist you in finding the best opportunities in local government for capitalizing on being a woman-owned business.

Where to Begin

As mentioned in the previous chapter on state government, I suggest that you begin your research with your local area. The familiarity and access to people and information will make the research process easier.

Once you have completed the research on your local area, it is best to have a plan for expanding your exploration into other areas so that you build on your efforts and findings.

There are usually similarities in geographic areas just because of proximity. The fact that the same state laws apply to all local government entities within that state means that there will definitely be similarities for all like bodies in that particular state.

To expand your local government research you can:

- Research local government entities, in surrounding geographic areas widening the circle until you have researched all the areas that you can physically and logically serve.
- Conduct research in areas where you have additional presence such as an office, plant or sales person.
- Conduct research in areas where you have existing customers/clients.
- Conduct research in areas that you know have conditions/situations that create a need for your specific products or services.

Note: Be sure you have determined the best local government entities for your products or services before you do any research. For example, if your target is law enforcement, you do not need to set your sights on a town that does not have a police department, but contracts with the county sheriff.

You do not necessarily need to expand your research state by state. As a matter of fact, you may want to move to areas in bordering states before expanding to some areas in your own state. The best plan for expanding research is a logical one. Here are some considerations that will help you determine where to most effectively expand your research:

- Can you more efficiently service clients/customers in cities and counties just across the boundary into the bordering state, than on the other side of your home state?

❑ Do situations, conditions, and needs for local government entities in bordering states create more of a need for your products or services than in other parts of your own state? (That is, you provide a product or service that is primarily used by public works departments in mountainous areas. Your state has an area that is part of a multi-state mountain region. Your state also has a beach or port area. Your research time to identify and qualify prospects would, of course, be better spent in the mountainous areas of the nearby states than in the beach/port area of your own state.)

❑ Make sure that the expansion of the local government portion of your business is compatible with your overall business plan.

Policy and Philosophy

When you are determining which local government entities are the best prospects, you will need to measure their commitment to the support and use of woman-owned businesses, especially the *use of.*

Note: Most local government entities are currently using the acronym W/MBE (woman/minority business enterprise), although some use MBE or minority business enterprise as an all-inclusive term. Some do not classify women as minorities; however, this is not very common.

The policy is an important initial indicator of the entity's level of commitment. It is a reflection of the philosophy and the basis for action. There are really three categories of policy:

❑ Most local government entities have a policy not to discriminate against W/MBEs (woman/minority business enterprises).

☐ Many have published statements about the use of W/MBEs that uses words such as: include, encourage, ensure use of, and maximize.

☐ Some have actual goals, commitments, or requirements for the use of W/MBEs.

You should start your research with the last one on this list. The other two may still be good prospects, but the ones that have actual measurements are the best. One of the good things about W/MBE Policies is that the more important they are to the local government entity, the easier it is to find the information.

The Website of the entity is the best place to begin your research. Usually you will find the policy in one of these sections:

☐ Purchasing or procurement

☐ Community development

☐ Economic development

☐ M/WBE or minority business development (occasionally under small business development)

The policy will normally include such things as:

☐ Qualifications for W/MBEs (woman/minority-owned businesses).

☐ How qualifying businesses will be identified (that is, a certification process, self-declaration, and so on).

☐ How the entity will support and facilitate W/MBE participation in procurement.

☐ Goals (if there are any) for the use of W/MBE by the local government entity and its prime contractors.

☐ Requirements and incentives for the use of minority businesses.

As this book has stated in previous chapters, a policy is only as good as the philosophy that supports it and the people who implement it. The philosophy has to do with the attitude and approach. If the policy was established because of a state law and really doesn't go any further than to assert that W/MBEs will not be discriminated against, then the philosophy is probably one of compliance with the law, but not necessarily commitment to action. Also, if the people implementing the policy do not feel and show a commitment to the use of W/MBEs, then the scenario is not the best one for capitalizing on being a woman-owned business. The philosophy is an important factor in determining the best prospects. The philosophy is not usually stated or published but is demonstrated in the implementation of the policy:

Policy Implementation

A policy is only as helpful as its implementation. When you are doing your research you cannot assume you have found a good prospect just because they have a policy and the policy uses the appropriate words. You must determine how the process and people make that policy a reality. This section provides some guidance on taking your research beyond the policy and philosophy.

Some of the typical implementation components or indicators are listed below. These are measures of the true commitment.

- ☐ Person, office, or department to support and promote the use of W/MBEs (or in some cases small business in general).
- ☐ A vendor list or database that specifies that a registered vendor is woman owned.

- ❑ RFPs (Request for Proposals), bids, and quotes state that woman-owned businesses are "encouraged" to submit.

- ❑ Reporting requirements on the use of woman-owned businesses (or at least W/MBEs) and publication of the reports.

- ❑ Advertisement of opportunities in publications and locations that cater to woman-owned businesses (or all MBEs).

- ❑ Actions that promote the use of W/MBEs (that is, trade fairs, matchmaking events, training, and so on).

- ❑ Awards for the use and/or support of W/MBEs.

The number of municipalities and counties that establish some type of person, office, or department to implement the policy for the use and support of W/MBEs is increasing. That person, office or department may be associated with purchasing/procurement, economic development, or community development. Neither of these associations is necessarily better than the others. The association, however, is an indicator of the local government entity's approach. For instance if W/MBE comes under purchasing/procurement then the focus is likely on "use." If community or economic development includes W/MBE then the focus is probably on "growth" of the W/MBEs. This information can provide you with a better understanding of the local government entity and assist you in not only prioritizing your research and grading your prospects, but it will also help you market your products and services to the entity. Normally, if a local government entity has a person/office/department for W/MBE, information on it will be accessible on the entity's Website.

If a local government entity keeps a list or database of woman-owned businesses it normally allows registration online or at least provides a form on its Website that you can print, fill-in, and mail. The registration will generally require some type of certification that you fit criteria; more information on certification is provided in Chapter 11.

The reporting requirements and the published reports are really statements of accountability. This information is another indicator of the level of commitment and the effectiveness of the policy implementation.

If the local government entity holds trade fairs, matchmaking events, or orientation sessions on "doing business with..." then this probably makes that entity a good prospect because they are doing some of the work for you. These occasions allow you to do a lot of research on prospects and opportunities in a very expedited and personalized method.

Direct Selling

To identify and qualify the best local government entities for your business it helps to have some understanding of the procurement/purchasing process so that you can find the opportunities and the buying trends. The following information is designed to help you gain that understanding and find the opportunities for both immediate and long term.

Each local government entity has its own set of rules; however, there are some common aspects. Some of those are:

- ❐ The rules are law and are established by the governing board (council, board, commissioners, and so on).
- ❐ Everyone in the local government entity must follow the rules precisely.
- ❐ The procurement/purchasing person or department is usually the "rules administrator."

- ☐ The dollar amount of the bid or project determines the exact process.

- ☐ Some local government entities post contract awards (winning bidder) on their Websites; they will often provide notification of the contract award to those who bid. Or you can request the contract award information.

When doing research it is important to know that local government entities and school districts often use the term "subcontracting" to mean "outsourcing." This is because the entity considers contracting with a company to provide such services as IT, facilities maintenance, and human resources as "subcontracting." This type of "subcontracting" may still be an opportunity for you, but it is really direct selling. So, be sure to look at subcontracting opportunities even if you are only interested in selling directly.

You will want to spend some time exploring the local government entity's Website and information in order to determine if that entity is a good prospect for you. This information will help you decide if proposing and providing services/products is feasible and cost effective for you. This research will also assist you in determining which specific departments, offices, and projects are good prospects. Here are some examples of areas you will want to explore and the information/understanding you will gain:

- ☐ The purchasing/procurement Web pages will likely provide:

  - ▪ Staff contact information and the guidelines for interacting with them (that is, "you must submit all questions by e-mail")

  - ▪ Levels and rules of competition (that is, procurements more than $25,000 must be done by sealed bid)

- Evaluation guidelines
- Payment terms
- Incentives and tax credits
- Standard contract requirements and language. (This is vital in determining if you can meet the requirements and if you can afford the expense of meeting the requirements for such things as insurance and bonding.
- Opportunities—Invitation for bids, request for proposals, and so on—provide information on the current needs and buying trends and immediate opportunities.
- Existing contracts, information on buying trends, amounts spent for goods and services (clues to budgets) and the entity's prime contractors (more information on prime contractors is covered in the subcontracting section of this chapter on page 86).

☐ If the entity has a person/office/department for woman/minority business development and support its Web pages provide helpful information such as:

- Projects or departments that are seeking minority vendors.
- Special programs, events, and opportunities.
- Reports on the goals and the actual dollars spent.

■ Changes in policies, goals, programs, and so on.

■ "How to do business with" guidance and training notices.

A suggested general process for conducting research to identify valid local government entity targets for your business is provided in the following pages.

Process for Gathering and Analyzing Information on Local Government Prospects

Question	Next Step	Tips/Notes
What are the local government entities in my geographical area?	Once you have identified the entities move on to the next question.	This chapter provides you a list of possibilities.
Which of the entities on the list have need for my products or services?	Move on to the next question for each of the entities on the narrowed list.	
Does the local government entity have a published policy on the use and support of women-owned businesses or W/MBEs?	If yes, move on to the next step. If no, but the entity does have a small-business development program then use that angle. If the entity does not have any type of related policy or program move them to the bottom of your list to possibly pursue with a totally different angle.	

Question	Next Step	Tips/Notes
Does the entity have a specified goal for the amount of money to spend with woman-owned businesses?	If yes, move on to the next question. If no, but they have a goal for the use of minority-owned businesses that includes woman-owned businesses continue on to the next step. If the entity does not have any goals for woman- or minority-owned businesses then consider a different approach if you wish to try to do business with this entity.	
Does the entity have current projects related to my products/services?	If yes, move on to the next step. If no, research further to determine the buying trends and plans.	Use the information in this chapter to find the current opportunities.
Does the entity have need of my products/services in a geographic area I can serve?	If yes, take the steps to bid or propose. If no, monitor for future opportunities	Set up a plan/schedule for monitoring opportunities.
Does the identified entity have a designated person to work with woman-owned businesses (or minority businesses, or even small businesses)?	Make note, this is an important qualifying and prioritizing fact.	

Question	Next Step	Tips/Notes
Does the identified entity have a history of awarding contracts to woman-owned businesses?	Make note, this is an important qualifying and prioritizing fact.	Use the information in this chapter to research the appropriate Websites.
Are opportunities with the identified entity more likely direct with my company or are they more likely subcontracting opportunities?	If the opportunities are more likely direct then move to the next question. If the opportunities are more likely subcontracting then skip to the analysis process for subcontracting.	Identifying and qualifying subcontracting opportunities are covered in the second part of this chapter, beginning on page 86.
After gathering information on five to 10 local government entities within a valid target area analyze and rank them according to the previous questions.	This should be your first list of prospects to contact for selling direct. Once you have made initial contact to each of these, you will be in the next phase of marketing with them. At that point, you should restart the identification and qualification process with new potential prospects within an area. At the same time, you should be looking at additional areas so you can begin the process of identifying specific agencies, departments, institutions.	Remember that in an effective marketing plan you will always have several prospects in each phase. Marketing strategy is covered in Chapter 12.

Subcontracting

As with state government there are two potential targets to identify and qualify—the local government entity itself and the prime contractors of that entity. However, prime contractors are not as clearly identified for local government entities as they are for state governments.

Some local government entities do have programs/efforts to promote the use of woman- and minority-owned businesses as subcontractors by prime contractors. Just as direct selling the type of program/effort depends on the policy, philosophy, and implementation.

Some of the ways that local government entities promote the use of minority subcontractors (including women) are:

- ☐ Contract requirement condition that prime contractors use or make a "good faith effort" to use minority subcontractors. Some local government entities have established guidelines and measurements for what constitutes a "good faith effort." The prime contractor is usually required to do one or both of the following:
  - ■ Submit a utilization or subcontracting plan.
  - ■ Show proof of contracts or attempts to obtain minority subcontractors.

- ☐ Some local government entities only have minority subcontractor programs for construction projects; but usually these programs are strong and the requirements of prime contractors are strictly enforced.

If a local entity does not have some type of program to promote the use of minority subcontractors that does not mean that there are no subcontracting opportunities; it simply means that you are on your own to find those opportunities.

Note: Many purchasing staffers with local government entities have told me that small businesses usually do not win a bid because they cannot meet all the requirements of the project such as capability, insurance, or equipment. They also say that if the small business would be willing to subcontract or partner with other businesses, they could get a portion of the business. The old saying, "a piece of the pie is better than nothing" might be the best philosophy here.

Once you have determined that a local government is a good target for your business, you want to move on to identify prime contractors and determine which ones are true prospects.

Unfortunately, most local government entities are not set up to easily provide specifics on their prime contractors. You will have to do some research that usually will involve talking with the personnel involved in purchasing/procurement. Although this may be time consuming, it does give you an opportunity to make your business known to them and begin a relationship. The information you are seeking is normally "public information" meaning it is not confidential and must be provided to anyone requesting it. Below are some suggested methods for identifying prime contractors:

- ❒ Existing contracts with a local government entity identify businesses that do get contracts with local government. These contracts are rarely listed on a Website. Usually, the best approach is to tell the purchasing staffer that you are looking for subcontracting opportunities and would like to know who has their contract for the particular product or service you can complement—be very specific about the product or service. There may not be an opportunity for you to subcontract on an existing contract, but it is worth your time to contact that prime contractor and let them know about your company for future contracts with other local government entities.

- ❒ Contract awards are another source of information about prime contractors. Some local government entities post contract awards on their Websites.

Even if they do not post them, the local government entity does provide notification to bidders of
contract awards. If you bid on a project you will
know who won the contract. If you do not, you can
still find out by contacting the purchasing staffer
after the contract has been awarded. These prime
contractors are potential for current or future subcontracting opportunities. You will have to monitor the postings of opportunities and identify those
for which you can provide a portion of the products
or services in order to apply this research method.

☐ Go through at least part of the process of bidding or submitting a proposal. This will provide
you an opportunity to find out what businesses
are interested in the opportunity. One or more
of these may present a subcontracting or
partnering opportunity for you. The steps within
the bidding/proposal process that offer a chance
to identify a potential prime contractor are:

■ Sometimes the process requires a "statement of intent to bid" so that
addendums to the original request for
bid/proposal can be sent. Sometimes the
addendums will include a list of potential bidders/proposers. You can submit
a "statement of intent to bid" and get
on the distribution list so that you can
see what other companies are on the list.

■ For larger projects there is usually a
pre-bid meeting/conference—this is
an excellent opportunity to actually see
prospective prime contractors. It is
worth attending these meetings; even
if you do not intend to bid/propose, it
is still an opportunity for identification

and qualification of subcontracting prospects.

■ A request for bid/proposal may allow vendors to submit questions. You should participate in this even if you do not intend to propose, because this will allow you to see the questions (usually identified by vendor) and the answers. This is great information to use in your identification and qualification efforts. A vendor may expose their subcontracting needs in the questions they ask (that is, "Does the successful bidder have to do the installation?")

☐ Newspaper announcements about contract awards provide the name of the company that gets the contract. These announcements will normally be in the business section because the press release is submitted by the business that won the contract.

You will probably have to do additional research to qualify the prime contractors you have identified. Some of the things that will keep them from being a good prospect for you are:

☐ They can do everything in the contract themselves.

☐ They already have a partnership/subcontracting arrangement with another company. (This does not mean you should cross them completely off your list, they may be a prospect later.)

☐ They may have a subsidiary or sister company that does what you do.

☐ They may have a bad reputation for the way they treat subcontractors (be sure you find out the whole story before you cross them off your list).

❒   They may not really be qualified to bid/propose.

The following table provides a suggested process to determine if prime contractors are viable prospects.

Process for Gathering and Anlyzing Information on Local Government Subcontracting Prospects

Question	Next Step	Tips/Notes
Guide for Finding Prime Contractors With Existing Contracts		
Does the local government entity have existing contracts that involve your products/services?	If yes, move on to the next question.	There are tips in this chapter on page 87 about where and how to find the existing contracts.
Who is the prime contractor on the existing contract that involves your products/services?	Move on to the next question.	
Is this prime contractor capable of meeting all contract requirements alone?	If yes, move to the bottom of your list. If no, move on to next question.	
Does this prime contractor already have a subcontractor that provides the same products/services as you?	If yes, still consider contacting the prime contractor, but understand that this is a long-term possibility. If you do contact them, find out how strong the relationship and contract with the current subcontractor is. If no, move on to next step.	

Question	Next Step	Tips/Notes
Will this prime contractor benefit from using a woman-owned business (or minority-owned business if that classification includes women)?	If no, consider a different marketing angle to use if you want to pursue being a subcontractor to this prime contractor. If yes, contact them.	This chapter covers possible benefits on pages 87–89.
Is this prime contractor likely to bid on similar projects with other local government entities?	If no and you do not fit into this specific contract mark them off your list. If yes, then contact them about future opportunities.	

Guide for Finding Prime Contractors Through the Bidding Process on Local Government Contracts

Question	Next Step	Tips/Notes
Is there a bidding or RFP opportunity that involves your products/services?	If yes move on to the next question.	Tips on finding opportunities are covered in this chapter.
Is there a way to find out who the potential bidders or proposing vendors are?	If yes, move on to the next question.	Tips on obtaining this information are provided in this chapter.
Are the bidders or proposing vendors capable of meeting all the contract/project requirements?	If no, move on to the next question. If yes, move them to the bottom of your list and consider contacting them for future subcontracting opportunities.	

Question	Next Step	Tips/Notes
Does this prime contractor already have a subcontractor that provides the same products/services as you?	If no, move on to the next question. If yes, still consider contacting the prime contractor, but understand that this is a long-term possibility. If you do contact them, find out how strong the relationship and contract with the current subcontractor is.	
Would the bidder or proposing vendor benefit from using a woman-owned business as a subcontractor?	If yes, they are likely a target for you. If no, consider contacting them using a different marketing angle than the woman-owned angle.	This chapter covers possible benefits on pages 77–78.
Are you familiar enough with the bidder or proposing vendor to know if they would be a good partner?	If yes, contact. If no, do additional research before contacting them.	Good sources for additional information include: the company's Website and the pre-bid meeting.
Is this prime contractor likely to bid on similar projects with other local government entities?	If no, and you do not fit into this specific contract mark them off your list. If yes, then contact them about future opportunities.	

Question	Next Step	Tips/Notes
The following questions are designed to help you evaluate the potential prospect and do not necessarily build on each other.		
Does the prime contractor/bidder/ proposing vendor have a history of subcontracting with woman-owned businesses?	If yes, enhances your chances.	Remember that this book is about capitalizing on being woman-owned, not fighting causes. If convenience or something similar is the reason there is no history of using woman-owned businesses this may still be a valid prospect.
Is the local government entity involved in the bidding/RFP project struggling to meet their goal for the use of woman-owned businesses?	If yes, enhances your chances.	The office/department responsible for implementing the entity's minority business policy normally publishes reports. Other advice on finding answers to this question is provided in this chapter on page 78.
Are there other qualified woman-owned businesses registered in the area able to provide the same products/services as you?	If not, your chances increase.	Remember that a business must be certified by the state (or other entity they accept) in order to meet the subcontracting requirements.

Question	Next Step	Tips/Notes
Does the prime contractor/bidder/proposing vendor have a designated diversity contact (small business liaison, minority bus-developer, and so on) or is the listed contact more general in nature (purchaser, project manager, and so on).	This does not necessarily increase or decrease your chances, but it does provide you some insight for your dealings with the prospect.	You will probably have to investigate the company to find this answer.

Note: You should be evaluating and contacting prospects for direct and subcontracting simultaneously. It often happens that when you are researching or prospecting for one track you find an opportunity in a different track.

Chapter 7

Identifying and Qualifying Prospects:
STATE-SUPPORTED EDUCATION

State-supported education institutions are governed by the same procurement/purchasing rules as state government agencies, departments, and institutions; therefore, it is very important to understand a state's laws and rules. This chapter will cover things specific to state-supported education, so I recommend that you read the chapter on state government before proceeding with this chapter.

Once you have determined that a state has a strong commitment to the use and support of woman-owned businesses, you can begin to look at the specific education institutions and organizations in that state. The typical institutions and organizations are:

❐ Universities and colleges
❐ Community and/or technical colleges
❐ Oversight organization (that is, commission on higher education, state community/technical college board, and so on)
❐ Department or board of education
❐ Governor's schools (usually for arts, humanities, math, or science)

❑ Special schools (that is, school for the deaf and blind, state charter schools)
❑ Schools that are part of the correction system

In the following pages you will find information that will assist you in determining which state supported institutions and organizations provide you the best opportunities for capitalizing on the fact that you are a woman-owned business.

Where to Begin

If you have determined that your home state is a good prospect for woman-owned businesses, then you should start with the state supported institutions and organizations there. Familiarity and access to people that can help you will expedite your research.

Once you have completed the research on state supported education in your home state you can move on to other states, but you should have a plan for expanding your research. The first step in expanding your research is to identify and qualify the state as an appropriate prospect as outlined in Chapter 5.

Policy and Philosophy

The first step is to determine if a state-supported institution or organization has a published policy for the use of woman-owned businesses. If the state has a policy then the institution or organization is governed by that policy; however, institutions/organizations that have their own policy and publish it are the best prospects. Normally an institution/organization's policy is focused on the use of woman- and minority-owned businesses. The policy will usually include:

❑ Who qualifies
❑ How qualifying businesses will be identified (that is, a certification process, self-declaration, and so on.)
❑ Why there is a policy

❏ Acknowledgment that minority businesses have historically been restricted from, or hampered in, participation in free enterprise

❏ Quantitative goals, if there are any, for the use of minority businesses by the institution or organization

❏ Guidelines for prime contractors in the use of woman- and minority-owned businesses as subcontractors

All education institutions may be eventual prospects for your business. However, some will be more favorable for you than others. There is a guide on page 101 to help you determine the best prospects for you.

As stated in previous chapters, it is important to remember that even the most strongly stated policy is only as effective as the people who implement it. When researching state-supported education entities as prospects, it is essential to also understand the philosophy. The philosophy is the way the entity approaches this aspect of doing business. If the policy is the one established by the state, but the education entity's faculty and staff do not feel a commitment to carrying out the policy then the scenario is not the best one for capitalizing on being a woman-owned business. This is an important criterion in determining the best prospects for you. The philosophy is not usually stated or published but can be seen in the following:

❏ Designation of a person within the procurement/ purchasing department to work with and identify minority-owned businesses, including WOBs

❏ Reporting requirements for the use of minority businesses

❏ Requirement of prime contractors for the use of minority businesses

❏ Activities that promote the use of minority businesses (that is, trade fairs, matchmaking events, training, and so on)

- ☐ Accountability by departments and prime contractors for the use of minority businesses

Note: Refer back to Chapter 5 for additional information on state government as a whole.

Policy Implementation

Implementation of the policy is the true measure of commitment and an important indicator for your prospects of doing business with the education entities. Do not assume that you have found a promising prospect just because they have a policy and the policy uses the appropriate words. The next step is to determine how the process and people make the policy a reality. This section provides some guidance on taking your research beyond the policy and philosophy.

Usually the implementation will be managed by the office/ department responsible for procurement. The size of the education entity will likely dictate if they have a designated person or persons to work with woman- and minority-owned businesses. Sometimes the policy will include a statement that establishes the position of minority business liaison. However, even if there is not a designated person, the education entity may still work very hard to be sure that woman- and minority-owned businesses have solid opportunities. Some of indicators are:

- ☐ Reputation (if they have won any awards, what minority businesses say about them)
- ☐ Actions and activities (such as networking and matchmaking events, newsletters, and development workshops)
- ☐ Attitude (what they say and if it matches what they do, if they are in the helping or telling mode)
- ☐ Areas of concentration (if they focus on a particular segment of the minority business community)

❐ Inclusion of woman-owned businesses in their efforts to provide opportunities to minority-owned businesses.

Most states require that woman and minority businesses be certified in order to qualify for use by the state-supported education entities and their prime contractors in meeting the set goals. The office/department that implements the state's overall policy normally is responsible for certifying the woman, minority and/or small businesses. Certifications are covered in Chapter 11.

Direct Selling

It is important to have some understanding of the procurement/purchasing process of a state-supported education entity, so that you can find the best opportunities. The following information is designed to help you gain that understanding and find the opportunities both immediate and long term.

Common rules/procedures:

❐ The rules are law and are established by the state legislature and therefore apply to state-supported education.

❐ All rules must be followed precisely.

❐ The procurement/purchasing office or department is usually the "rules administrator."

❐ All opportunities more than a specific dollar threshold (set by each state, but typically any solicitation valued at $10,000 or more) will be posted on a Website for the state and/or the education entity.

❐ Contract awards (winning bidder) will probably be posted on the entity's Website.

❐ There is a vendor registration process (usually online is preferred) that allows potential vendors to place on record specific information about their business and its products or services.

You will want to further investigate the Website and information in order to determine if a state-supported education entity is a good prospect for you. This information will help you decide if proposing and providing services/products is feasible and cost effective. Here are some examples of things you will want to explore and the information/understanding you will gain:

- ❐ Staff contact information and the guidelines for interacting with them (that is, "you must submit all questions by email")
- ❐ Levels and rules of competition (that is procurements more than $25,000 must be done by sealed bid)
- ❐ Preferences (that is, a preference of X percent is given to state resident vendors over non-state resident vendors)
- ❐ Evaluation guidelines
- ❐ Payment terms
- ❐ Contract examples will provide standard contract requirements and language. This is vital in determining if you can meet the requirements and if you can afford the expense of meeting the requirements. The contract sections will likely include such things as:
    - ■ Insurance
    - ■ Indemnification
    - ■ Bond requirements
    - ■ Legal requirements such as: force majure, save harmless, default, and termination
- ❐ Opportunities—invitation for bids, request for proposals, and so on—provide information on the current needs and buying trends.

❑ Contract award notifications provide information on buying trends, amounts spent for goods and services (clues to budgets), and the entity's prime contractors (more information on prime contractors is covered in the subcontracting section of this chapter beginning on page 103).

❑ The specific Websites of departments and institutions furnish procurement/purchasing information on important issues and trends.

A suggested general process for conducting research to identify valid state-supported targets for your business is provided in the following pages.

Process for Gathering and Analyzing Information on State-Supported Education Projects

Question	Next Step	Tips/Notes
Does the entity have a published policy on the use and support of women-owned businesses?	If yes, move on to the next question. If no, does the entity have a minority business use policy, and if so does it include women-owned businesses? If yes, move on to the next step. If the entity does have a minority-use policy that does not include woman-owned businesses then move on to the next entity on your list and consider a different approach if you wish to try to do business with this entity.	

Question	Next Step	Tips/Notes
Does the entity have a specified goal for the amount of money to spend with woman-owned businesses?	If yes, move on to the next question. If no, but they have a goal for use of minority-owned businesses that includes woman-owned businesses; continue on to the next step. If the entity does not have any goals for minority-owned business use then consider a different approach if you wish to try to do business with this entity.	
Does entity have current projects related to my products/services?	If yes, move on to the next step. If no, research further to determine the buying trends and plans.	Use the information in this section to research the Websites of the entity agencies, departments, and institutions.
Does entity have need of my products/services in a geographic area I can serve?	If yes, move on to the next question. If no, move entity down your list for reconsideration when your service area and the entity's needs are a better match.	Use the information in this section to research the Websites of the entity agencies, departments and institutions.
Does the identified entity have a designated person to work with woman-owned businesses (or minority businesses, or even small businesses)?	This will help you in prioritizing, because it makes the marketing process easier.	

Question	*Next Step*	*Tips/Notes*
Does the identified entity have a history of awarding contracts to woman-owned businesses?	Make note, this is an important qualifying and prioritizing fact.	Use the information in this section to research the Websites of the entity agencies, departments, and institutions.
Are opportunities with this entity more likely direct with my company or are they more likely subcontracting opportunities?	If the opportunities are more likely direct then move to the next question. If the opportunities are more likely subcontracting then skip to the analysis process for subcontracting.	Identifying and qualifying subcontracting opportunities are covered in the second part of this chapter begining on the bottom of this page.
After gathering information on four to eight entities within a valid target state, analyze and rank them according to the previous questions.	This should be your first list of prospects to contact for selling direct. Once you have made initial contact to each of these, you will be in the next phase of marketing with them. At that point, you should restart the identification and qualification process with new potential prospects within an entity.	Remember that in an effective marketing plan you will always have several prospects in each phase. We are only covering the initial phase in this chapter, beginning at the bottom of this page.

Subcontracting

There are actually two potential targets to identify and qualify—the state supported education entity itself and the prime contractors of that entity.

Most states have some type of program/effort to promote the use of woman- and minority-owned businesses as subcontractors by prime contractors that apply to state-supported education entities. Some of the ways that states promote the use of minority subcontractors (including women) are:

❑ Encouragement or requirement of prime contractors use or make a "good faith effort" to use minority subcontractors. Guidelines and measurements for what constitutes a "good faith effort" usually include one or both of the following:

■ Submit a utilization or subcontracting plan.

■ Show proof of contracts or attempts to obtain minority subcontractors.

❑ Some entities post subcontracting opportunities on the procurement/purchasing Websites.

❑ Some entities only have minority subcontractor programs for construction projects; but usually these programs are strong and the requirements of prime contractors are strictly enforced.

Once you have determined that a state-supported entity is a good target for your business, you want to move on to identify prime contractors and determine which ones are true prospects.

Information on the prime contractors can be found in the following places:

❑ Existing contracts with the entity

❑ Posting of contract awards, which are usually on the procurement/purchasing Web pages. The notice of award will provide a general label of the product or service (that is, laptop computers, janitorial service, or temporary staffing) and the name and contact information of the prime contractor.

However, the notice of award does not usually provide any details or specifics. The best method for identifying projects for which you may be a subcontractor candidate is to follow the trail in this manner:

- Monitor the postings of opportunities and identify those for which you can provide a portion of the products or services

- Watch the awards Website to see which vendor actually gets the contract

- Even if there is not an opportunity for you to subcontract on this specific contract, you have identified a business that qualifies as a prime contractor

❐ Go through at least part of the process of bidding or submitting a proposal. This will provide you an opportunity to find out what businesses are interested in the opportunity. One or more of these may present a subcontracting opportunity for you. The steps within the bidding/proposal process that offer a chance to identify a potential prime contractor are:

- Sometimes the process requires a "statement of intent to bid" so that addendums to the original request for bid/proposal can be sent. Sometimes the addendums will include a list of potential bidders/proposers.

- For larger projects there is usually a pre-bid meeting/conference—this is an excellent opportunity to actually see prospective prime contractors. It is worth attending these meetings, even if you do not intend to bid/propose, it is still an excellent opportunity for identification and qualification of subcontracting prospects.

- A request for bid/proposal may allow vendors to submit questions. You should participate in this even if you do not intend to propose because this will allow you to see the questions (usually identified by vendor) and the answers. This is great information to use in your identification and qualifying efforts—a vendor may expose their subcontracting needs in the questions they ask.

❐ Newspaper announcements about contract awards.

You will need to do additional research to qualify the prime contractors you have identified. Just because they provide products or services that are related to yours, does not mean they are a true prospect. Some of the possible difficulties are:

❐ They may be able to do everything themselves.

❐ They already have a partnership/subcontracting arrangement with another company. (This does not mean you should cross them completely off your list, they may be a prospect later.)

❐ They may have a subsidiary or sister company that does what you do.

❐ They may have a bad reputation for the way they treat subcontractors (be sure you find out the whole story before you cross them off your list).

❐ They may not really be qualified to bid/propose.

The following table provides a suggested process to determine if prime contractors are viable prospects.

Process for Gathering and Analyzing Information in State-Supported Education Subcontracting Prospects

Question	Next Step	Tips/Notes
Guide for Finding Prime Contractors With Existing Contracts		
Does the entity have existing contracts that involve my products/ services?	If yes, move on to the next question.	There are tips in this chapter about where and how to find the existing contracts.
Who is the prime contractor on the existing contract that involves my products/services?	Move on to the next question.	
Is this prime contractor capable of meeting all contract requirements alone?	If yes, move to the bottom of your list. If no, move on to next question.	
Does this prime contractor already have a subcontractor that provides the same products/services as you?	If yes, still consider contacting the prime contractor, but understand that this is a long-term possibility. If you do contact them, find out how strong the relationship and contract with the current subcontractor is. If no, move on to next step.	

Question	Next Step	Tips/Notes
Will this prime contractor benefit from using a woman-owned business (or minority-owned business if that classification includes women)?	If no, consider a different marketing angle to use if you want to pursue being a subcontractor to this prime contractor. If yes, contact them.	This chapter covers possible benefits.

Guide for Finding Prime Contractors Through the Bidding Process.

Question	Next Step	Tips/Notes
Is there a bidding or RFP opportunity that involves my products/services?	If yes, move on to the next question.	Tips on finding opportunities are covered in this chapter on page 100.
Is there a way to find out who the potential bidders or proposing vendors are?	If yes, move on to the next question.	Tips on obtaining this information are provided in this chapter on page 104.
Are the bidders or proposing vendors capable of meeting all the contract/project requirements?	If no, move on to the next question. If yes, move them to the bottom of your list and consider contacting them for future subcontracting opportunities.	

Question	Next Step	Tips/Notes
Does this prime contractor already have a subcontractor that provides the same products/services as you?	If no, move on to the next question. If yes, still consider contacting the prime contractor, but understand that this is a long-term possibility. If you do contact them, find out how strong the relationship and contract with the current subcontractor is.	
Would the bidder or proposing vendor benefit from using a woman-owned business as a subcontractor?	If yes, they are likely a target for you. If no, consider contacting them using a different marketing angle than the woman-owned angle.	This chapter covers possible benefits on pages 97–98.
Are you familiar enough with the bidder or proposing vendor to know if they would be a good partner?	If yes, contact. If no, do additional research before contacting them.	Good sources for additional information include: the company's Website, the entity's existing contract list, and the pre-bid meeting.

Question	Next Step	Tips/Notes
The following questions are designed to help you evaluate the potential prospect and do not necessarily build on each other.		
Does the prime contractor/bidder/proposing vendor have a history of subcontracting with woman-owned businesses?	If yes, enhances your chances.	Remember that this book is about capitalizing on being woman-owned, not fighting causes. If convenience or something similar is the reason there is no history of using woman-owned businesses this may still be a valid prospect.
Is the entity involved in the bidding/RFP project struggling to meet their goal for the use of woman-owned businesses?	If yes, enhances your chances.	
Are there other qualified woman-owned businesses registered with the entity able to provide the same products/services as you?	If not, your chances increase.	Remember that a business must be certified by the state (or other entity they accept) in order to meet the subcontracting requirements.
Does prime contractor/bidder/proposing vendor have a designated diversity contact (small business liaison, minority bus developer, and so on) or is the listed contact more general in nature (purchaser, project manager, etc.)?	This does not necessarily increase or decrease your chances, but it does provide you some insight for your dealings with the prospect.	You will probably have to investigate the company to find this answer.

Note: You should be evaluating and contacting prospects for direct and subcontracting simultaneously. It often happens that when you are researching or prospecting for one track you find an opportunity in a different track.

Chapter 8

Identifying and Qualifying Prospects:

PRIVATE EDUCATION

Private education institutions are under no obligation to have any type of plan for supplier diversity or woman/minority business usage. If they have such a plan it is because their management (board, president, procurement staff) feels that it is the right thing to do. The two factors that usually play into that decision are:

❒ Social consciousness about ensuring that woman and minority businesses have equal access to opportunities

❒ Understanding that the institution benefits from a diverse vendor base.

Private education institutions can include:

❒ Universities and colleges

❒ K–12 schools and academies

❒ Associated organizations

In the following pages you will find information that will assist you in determining which private institutions and organizations provide you the best opportunities for capitalizing on the fact that you are a woman-owned business.

Where to Begin

As suggested in other chapters, starting the identifying and qualifying research with your local area or state makes your search more efficient because of familiarity and accessibility. Once you have completed the research in your home state you can move on to other states, but you should have a plan for expanding your research.

You may be surprised at how many private education institutions and organizations exist in your local area and throughout the country. The schools, especially college level, are often called independent colleges and universities. Elementary and secondary/high schools (K–12 level) are usually classified as private. An organization's name will likely match the type of institution it supports.

There are also private education institutions that are specific for a profession, such as chiropractor, massage therapist, IT professional, nurse, medical occupation, and many more. The institution may offer certifications or diplomas in their programs of study, but may not offer actual degrees, such as associates or bachelors.

Here are some places to begin your search:

- Local phone directories (both printed and online)
- Online searches using the following key words:
    - Private school
    - Private academy
    - Private college
    - Military academy
    - Independent school
    - Independent academy
    - Independent college
    - Independent university
    - Christian school

- Specific religion (that is, Catholic, Presbyterian, Baptist, Episcopal, and so on) school
- Specific religion college
- Specific religion university
- Specific profession or type of profession (that is, medical, Chiropractor, technical, and so on) school or training

❑ Local or state associations for:

- Independent colleges and universities
- Private academies and K–12 schools
- Religious affiliated private schools
- Specific professions (that is, veterinary technician, medical records, criminal justice, and so on.)

❑ Newspapers (usually education and sports sections will include news on private as well as public schools)

Policy and Philosophy

If a private education institution has a policy for supplier diversity or the use of woman/minority-owned businesses, it may be as simple as that it will not discriminate. This type of policy makes them a more likely prospect than an institution that has no policy, but not as good a candidate as one that actually sets a goal.

An institution may not publish its policy on its Website or in its materials, but this does not mean it does not have one. Remember that the Website is designed for the institutions clients, not thier vendors.

Because a policy is only as effective as the people implementing it carry it through, it is essential to find proof that the philosophy matches the policy. The philosophy is the way the institution approaches supplier diversity. If the policy is the one established by the administration, but the private education institution's buyers (procurement personnel, faculty, and staff) do not feel a commitment to carrying out the policy then this may be a fair candidate for capitalizing on being woman owned, but not necessarily the best. The philosophy is not usually stated but can be seen in the following:

❏ Designation of a person within the procurement/ purchasing department to identify and work with minority-owned businesses, including WOBs.

❏ Goals, especially with published results, for the use of WOBs.

❏ Requirement of prime contractors for the use of minority businesses.

❏ Opportunity to register as a woman-owned vendor.

❏ Activities that promote the use of minority businesses (that is, trade fairs, matchmaking events, training, and so on).

❏ Accountability by departments and prime contractors for the use of minority businesses.

In the case of private education institutions, there may be situations where there is not a policy, but there is a strong philosophy to use woman- and minority-owned businesses.

You will likely find that there is some consistency that can guide your research to be sure your time is spent effectively. This consistency is evidenced by the indication of a policy and/or philosophy. Some of the possibilities for consistency are:

❏ Type of institutions (for instance you might find that liberal arts colleges are more likely than technical/technology-related ones to use your products and services)

❏ A specific category (such as a military academy is a better candidate for you than a general private high school)

❐ Affiliation (a religious affiliation may make the institution a probable or non-probable candidate)
❐ Geographic area

Occasionally a private education institution will receive a public or private grant that requires they utilize woman/minority-owned businesses as vendors on the project being funded by the grant. This will take some indepth research to identify; however, because there are likely few, maybe no, other WOBs willing to do this research you could have a strong advantage. If you regularly watch the institution's Website and the local papers you will probably see the notice if a grant is received. Then you can research the granting entity or contact the person at the institution responsible for the funded project to find out about vendor opportunities and if there are any requirements for the type of vendors.

Policy Implementation

Implementation of the policy is an important indicator for your private education institution prospects. Be sure you do the research to determine if and how the process and people make the policy a reality. This section provides some help on doing that.

Usually the implementation will be managed by the office/department responsible for purchasing. The size of the private education institution will probably determine if they have a designated person or persons to work with woman- and minority-owned businesses. This makes it easier to leverage your woman-owned status; however, even if there is not a designated person, the private education institution may still make efforts to be sure that woman- and minority-owned businesses have equal access to opportunities. This is evidenced by such things as:

❐ Reputation (have they have won any awards, what minority businesses say about them)

- ❑ Attitude (what they say and if it matches what they do, they are in the helping or telling mode)
- ❑ Areas of concentration (they focus on a particular segment of the minority business community)
- ❑ Inclusiveness of woman-owned businesses in their efforts to provide opportunities to minority-owned businesses
- ❑ Membership in organizations that support woman/minority-owned businesses

Direct Selling

You will want to explore the private education institutions website to determine if it is a good prospect for you. This information will help you decide if proposing and providing services/products is feasible and cost effective. Here are some examples of things you will want to discover:

- ❑ Vendor or purchasing guidelines or rules
- ❑ Staff contact information
- ❑ Evaluation guidelines
- ❑ Payment terms
- ❑ Contract examples will provide standard contract requirements and language. This is important in determining if you can meet the requirements and if you can afford the expense of meeting the requirements. The contract sections will likely include such things as:
  - ■ Insurance
  - ■ Indemnification
  - ■ Bond requirements
  - ■ Legal requirements such as: force majure, save harmless, default, and termination

❏ Opportunities—invitation for bids, request for proposals, and so on—provide information on the current needs and buying trends.

❏ The specific Web pages of departments and programs furnish information on important issues, trends, and other things that affect the products and services they need.

A suggested general process for conducting research to identify private education targets for your business is provided in the following pages.

Process for Gathering and Analyzing Information on Private Education Prospects

Question	Next Step	Tips/Notes
Does the institution have a published policy on the use and support of women-owned businesses?	If yes, move on to the next question. If no, does the institution have a minority business use policy, and if so does it include women owned businesses? If yes, move on to the next step. If the institution does have a minority use policy that does not include woman-owned businesses then move on to the next institution on your list and consider a different approach if you wish to try to do business with this institution.	

Question	Next Step	Tips/Notes
Does the institution have a specified goal for the amount of money to spend with woman-owned businesses?	If yes, move on to the next question. If no, but they have a goal for use of minority-owned businesses that includes woman-owned businesses, continue on to the next step. If the institution does not have any goals for minority-owned business use then consider a different approach if you wish to try to do business with this institution.	
Does the institution have current projects related to my products/services?	If yes, move on to the next step. If no, research further to determine the buying trends and plans.	Use the information in this section to research the Web pages of the institution's departments and programs.
Does the identified institution have a designated person to work with woman-owned businesses (or minority businesses, or even small businesses)?	This will help you in prioritizing, because it makes the marketing process easier.	
Does the identified institution have a history of awarding contracts to woman-owned businesses?	Make note, this is an important qualifying and prioritizing fact.	

Question	Next Step	Tips/Notes
Are opportunities with this institution more likely direct with my company or are they more likely subcontracting opportunities?	If the opportunities are more likely direct, move to the next question. If the opportunities are more likely subcontracting, skip to the analysis process for subcontracting.	Identifying and qualifying subcontracting opportunities are covered in the second part of this chapter beginning below.
After gathering information on four to eight entities analyze and rank them according to the previous questions.	This should be your first list of prospects to contact for selling direct. Once you have made initial contact to each of these you will be in the next phase of marketing with them. At that point you should restart the identification and qualification process with new potential prospects.	Remember that in an effective Marketing Plan you will always have several prospects in each phase. We are only covering the initial phase in this chapter. Additional guidance is provided on marketing strategy in Chapter 12.

Subcontracting

There may be two potential targets to identify and qualify—the private education institution itself and its prime contractors.

Even if a private education institution has a policy and/or philosophy to use woman/minority-owned businesses they may not impose any requirements for such use on their prime contractors. However, even if there is not a requirement that prime contractors use W/MBEs, the prime contractors may feel that it gives them an advantage if the institution feels strongly about it. This is one of those things that will take some research, but could be profitable because most other businesses will not do the investigation. This research could also save you some time because:

- ☐ You will know where to concentrate your time.
- ☐ You can take advantage of an opportunity to get some business, but not have to take the lead in the bidding and project management.
- ☐ You will identify prime contractors that do work with private education institutions so that you can contact them about future opportunities. (Try to determine if they have any type of specialization or concentration on particular types, classification, or location so that you can better approach them or cross them off your list.)

Information on the prime contractors can be found in the following places:

- ☐ Existing contracts with the institution (this will only be on the Website if the institution is large).
- ☐ Newspaper announcements about contract awards.
- ☐ Talk with the procurement/purchasing staff or person and explain that you would like to do business with them, but realize that your size may make you a better subcontractor than prime contractor. Explain what you do and ask who their vendors are that provide related products or services. (The side benefit of this is that you may uncover a direct sell opportunity.)
- ☐ Where possible go through at least part of the process of bidding or submitting a proposal. This will provide you an opportunity to find out what businesses are interested in the opportunity. One or more of them may provide subcontracting

opportunities in the future. These are the steps within the bidding/proposal process that offer a chance to identify a potential prime contractor:

- For larger projects there is usually a pre-bid meeting/conference—this is an excellent opportunity to actually see prospective prime contractors. It is worth attending these meetings; even if you do not intend to bid/propose, it is still an excellent opportunity for identification and qualification of subcontracting prospects.

- A request for bid/proposal may allow vendors to submit questions. You should participate in this even if you do not intend to propose because this will allow you to see the questions (usually identified by vendor) and the answers. This is great information to use in your identification and qualifying efforts—a vendor may expose their subcontracting needs in the questions they ask.

❏ Newspaper announcements about contract awards. This is usually in the business section and is an announcement by the company winning the award.

You will need to do additional research to qualify the prime contractors you have identified. Just because an entity provides products or services that are related to yours, does not mean it is a true prospect. Some of the possible difficulties are:

❏ It may be able to do everything.
❏ It already has a partnership/subcontracting arrangement with another company. (This does not mean you should cross it off your list completely, they may be a prospect later.)

- ❑ It may have a subsidiary or sister company that does what you do.
- ❑ It may have a bad reputation for the way it treats subcontractors (be sure you find out the whole story before you cross it off your list).
- ❑ It may see no need to utilize woman-owned businesses in providing products or services to private education institutions.

The following table provides a suggested process to determine if prime contractors are viable prospects.

Process for Gathering and Analyzing Information on Private Education Subcontracting Prospects

Question	Next Step	Tips/Notes
Guide for Finding Prime Contractors With Existing Contracts		
Does the institution have existing contracts that involve my products/services?	If yes, move on to the next question.	There are tips in this chapter on page 122 about where and how to find the existing contracts.
Who is the prime contractor on the existing contract that involves my products/services?	Move on to the next question.	
Is this prime contractor capable of meeting all contract requirements alone?	If yes, move them to the bottom of your list. If no, move on to next question.	

Question	Next Step	Tips/Notes
Does this prime contractor already have a subcontractor that provides the same products/services as you?	If yes, still consider contacting the prime contractor, but understand that this is a long-term possibility. If you do contact them, find out how strong the relationship and contract with the current subcontractor is. If no, move on to next step.	
Will this prime contractor benefit from using a woman-owned business (or minority-owned business if that classification includes women)?	If no, consider a different marketing angle to use if you want to pursue being a subcontractor to this prime contractor. If yes, contact them.	

Guide for Finding Prime Contractors Through the Bidding Process

Question	Next Step	Tips/Notes
Is there a bidding or RFP opportunity that involves my products/services?	If yes, move on to the next question.	
Is there a way to find out who the potential bidders or proposing vendors are?	If yes, move on to the next question.	Tips on obtaining this information is provided in this chapter on page 123.

Question	Next Step	Tips/Notes
Are the bidders or proposing vendors capable of meeting all the contract/project requirements?	If no, move on to the next question. If yes, move them to the bottom of your list and consider contacting them for future subcontracting opportunities.	
Does this prime contractor already have a subcontractor that provides the same products/services as you?	If no, move on to the next question. If yes, still consider contacting the prime contractor, but understand that this is a long-term possibility. If you do contact them, find out how strong the relationship and contract with the current subcontractor are.	
Would the bidder or proposing vendor benefit from using a woman-owned business as a subcontractor?	If yes, they are likely a target for you. If no, consider contacting them using a different marketing angle than the woman-owned angle.	This chapter covers possible benefits.
Are you familiar enough with the bidder or proposing vendor to know if they would be a good partner?	If yes, contact. If no, do additional research before contacting them.	Good sources for additional information include: the company's Website, the institution's existing contract list, and the pre-bid meeting.

Question	Next Step	Tips/Notes
The following questions are designed to help you evaluate the potential prime contractor prospect and do not necessarily build on each other.		
Does the prime contractor/bidder/proposing vendor have a history of subcontracting with woman-owned businesses?	If yes, enhances your chances.	Remember that this book is about capitalizing on being woman-owned, not fighting causes. If convenience or something similar is the reason there is no history of using woman-owned businesses this may still be a valid prospect.
Is the institution involved in the bidding/RFP project struggling to meet their goal for the use of woman-owned businesses or does it have a reputation for using WOBs?	If yes, enhances your chances.	
Does the prime contractor/bidder/proposing vendor have a designated diversity contact (small business liaison, minority business developer, and so on) or is the listed contact more general in nature (purchaser, project manager, and so on)?	This does not necessarily increase or decrease your chances, but it does provide you some insight for your dealings with the prospect.	You will probably have to investigate the company to find this answer.

Note: You should be evaluating and contacting prospects for direct and subcontracting simultaneously. It often happens that when you are researching or prospecting for one track you find an opportunity in a different track.

Chapter 9

Identifying and Qualifying Prospects:
PUBLIC K–12 EDUCATION

Public K–12 education is administered by school districts. These districts vary in size, responsibility, and authority depending on both local and state government laws. However, most school districts have some common purchasing/procurement aspects. Although this book is not a study in school district organization or operation, it will cover some of the "rules" as they apply to opportunities for woman-owned businesses.

Things related to the use of woman/minority-owned businesses are usually centered in the purchasing/procurement area. Very few districts have development programs for woman, minority, or small businesses, although they may be involved in efforts/programs in their area.

Often the level of commitment to the use and support of woman/minority-owned businesses is directly related to the size of the district, or more specifically the size of their purchasing/procurement staff. School districts can vary in size from a hand full of schools to hundreds of schools. The purchasing/procurement staff parallels the size of the district. As a matter of fact, the purchasing/procurement function may merely be a part of a finance department staffer's responsibilities in a very small district. The smaller the district, and its purchasing/procurement staff, the less attention vendor diversity will get. This does not mean there are not opportunities, but it does place more responsibility on the woman-owned business to market their company and to remind the district of the goal or issue.

The size of a district may determine how many/much of something is purchased, but most districts have the same needs (that is, all districts need printer paper). School districts differ from local governments and other education institutions in this way: If one district has need of your products or services others likely will, too. This is not always true, but it is much more likely than with other potential customers or clients. This is because the requirements and regulations governing public K–12 education are more uniform throughout the nation than other public entities. So when doing the research for school district prospects, a woman-owned business may not have to determine if each individual district has a need for their products or services once they have made that determination for one or two districts. If your products or services are very specialized, though, that determination may have to be made on a district-by-district basis.

Once you have concluded that school districts are candidates for your products or services, you can begin to identify and qualify the ones that have a strong commitment to the use of woman-owned businesses. This chapter will help in that identification and qualification. As with other public entities covered in previous chapters, the philosophies and actions of school districts that affect their level of support and commitment are constantly changing because of:

- ❐ Change of elected officials (board, superintendent)
- ❐ Change of staff (finance or purchasing manager)
- ❐ Change in laws (procurement code, incentives, and so on)

❐ Receipt of grants or federal/state funds that have diversity requirements

Where to Begin

Even though any school district may be a potential prospect for you, it still makes sense to begin your research with your local area. The research process will be easier.

Once you have completed the research in your local and surrounding area it is best to have a plan for expanding your exploration into other areas so that you build on your efforts and findings.

Some approaches you can use to expand your school district research are:

❐ Research districts in surrounding geographic areas widening the circle until you have researched all the areas that you can physically and logically serve.

❐ Expand your research first within your own state and then in a state-by-state manner. This can be advantageous because of the laws, funding, trends, and so on, that will be common to all districts within a specific state.

❐ Conduct research in areas where you have additional presence such as an office, plant, or sales person.

❐ Conduct research in areas where you have existing customers/clients.

❐ Conduct research in areas where you want to grow your business.

❐ Make sure that the expansion of the K–12 portion of your business is compatible with your overall business plan.

Policy and Philosophy

When you are determining which school districts are the best prospects, you will need to measure their commitment to the support and, especially, the use of women-owned businesses.

Note: Most school districts are currently using the acronym W/MBE (woman/minority business enterprise), although some use MBE or minority business enterprise as an all-inclusive term. Some do not classify women as minorities; however, this is not very common.

The policy is an important initial indicator of the district's level of commitment. It is a reflection of the philosophy and the basis for action.

Schools districts are normally required by law to provide fair and equal opportunity to all vendors. They usually have a statement in the purchasing/procurement code (law) stating that woman- and minority-owned businesses shall be afforded the opportunity to participate fully in procurement. The code may go on to use such words as encourage, enhance, or assist in the statement about minority-owned businesses. Most districts include woman-owned in the minority-owned classification.

Some districts are required by state law to have goals for the use of woman/minority-owned businesses; some do so voluntarily. Many districts require their prime contractors to have goals for the use of woman/minority subcontractors.

You should start your research with the districts that have specific, measurable goals for the use of woman- or minority-owned businesses. Other districts may still be good prospects, but the ones that have actual measurements are the best for initial efforts.

The Website of the entity is the best place to begin your research. Usually you will find the policy in the purchasing or procurement section.

The policy will normally include such things as:

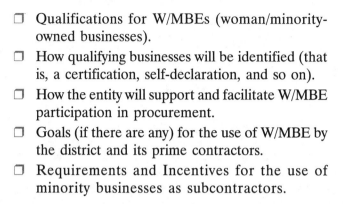

❒ Qualifications for W/MBEs (woman/minority-owned businesses).

❒ How qualifying businesses will be identified (that is, a certification, self-declaration, and so on).

❒ How the entity will support and facilitate W/MBE participation in procurement.

❒ Goals (if there are any) for the use of W/MBE by the district and its prime contractors.

❒ Requirements and Incentives for the use of minority businesses as subcontractors.

A district's policy is only as effective as the philosophy that supports it and the people who implement it. The philosophy is a reflection of the attitude and approach. If the policy was established because of a state or local law and is simply an assertion that there will be no discrimination against W/MBEs, then the philosophy is probably more about compliance with the law than about action. Also, if the people implementing the policy do not feel and show a commitment to the use of W/MBEs, then the scenario is not the best one for capitalizing on being a woman-owned business. As stated earlier in this chapter, many times the person responsible for purchasing/procurement also has other responsibilities and therefore, the time they have to spend on implementing the policy is limited. They will not break the law, but they probably are not in a position to "go the extra mile" either.

The philosophy is an important factor in determining the best prospects. The philosophy is not usually stated or published, but is demonstrated in the implementation of the policy. However, keep in mind that the philosophy may be dictated by staff and time constraints and not necessarily a reflection of the commitment to vendor diversity. Sometimes the lack of staff and time to handle an important matter provides an opportunity to aide the responsible person. In other words, if the person responsible for purchasing/procurement does not have time to pay close attention to the use of woman-owned businesses, you can position yourself to help them just by letting them know you exist and being there to call on for bids and quotes. Although this is really marketing advice, it is important to consider this when determining who is a prospect.

Policy Implementation

In qualifying prospects you should determine the effectiveness of the process and people who make that policy a reality. Here are some of the typical implementation components that are commitment indicators:

❑ Person, office, or department to support and promote the use of W/MBEs (or in some cases small business in general).

❑ A vendor list or database that indicates a registered vendor is woman-owned.

❑ RFPs (Request for Proposals), bids, and quotes state that woman-owned businesses are "encouraged" to submit.

❑ Reporting requirements on the use of woman-owned businesses (or at least W/MBEs) and publication of the reports.

❑ Advertisement of opportunities in publications and locations that cater to woman-owned businesses (or all MBEs).

❑ Participation in events that promote the use of W/MBEs (that is, trade fairs, matchmaking events, training, and so on).

❑ Awards for the use and/or support of W/MBEs.

One thing to remember in conducting research to qualify school district prospects is that its Website is designed to inform and aide students and parents, not vendors. Sometimes it is difficult to find information on vendor diversity or

W/MBEs. You may have to call or visit the purchasing/procurement department or person. If you do call or visit, it is best not to lead with a question about their diversity policy or actions. It is best to tell them you are seeking information about how to register as a vendor and do business with them, then ask if they have a guide for vendors. If they do not have a guide, get them to tell you about their requirements and weave your question about woman/minority-owned businesses into the conversation.

If a district keeps a list or database of woman-owned businesses they normally allow registration online or at least provide a form on their Website that you can print, fill-out, and mail to them. The registration will generally require some type of certification that you fit the criteria; more information on certification is provided in this book in Chapter 11.

If a district actually provides reports on their use of woman/minority-owned businesses, then this is an indication that they are holding themselves accountable. This is a measurement of the level of commitment and the effectiveness of the policy implementation.

If the district holds or participates in trade fairs, matchmaking events or orientation sessions on "doing business with..." then they are probably a good prospect because they are trying to make it easier to do business with them.

Direct Selling

As with local government entities, it helps to have some understanding of the procurement/purchasing process of school districts. The information that follows is designed to help you gain that understanding and find opportunities both immediate and long term.

School district's purchasing/procurement codes have some common aspects. Some of those are:

❏ The rules are law; some are established by the state and some by the local board.

❏ Everyone in the district must follow the rules precisely.

❏ The procurement/purchasing person or department is usually the "rules administrator."

❏ The dollar amount of the bid or project determines the exact process (that is, how many bidders are required, if the bids can be verbal, and so on).

One clarification that will help you in your research is that school districts and local government entities often use the term "subcontracting" to mean "outsourcing." They consider contracting with a company to provide such services as janitorial, cafeteria, and human resources as "subcontracting." Of course this may still be an opportunity, but it is really direct selling to the district. So, if even you are only interested in selling directly to the district you will still want to look at subcontracting opportunities.

You should begin your research on a district with its Website. The information on the site will help you decide if proposing and providing services/products is feasible and cost effective for you. You will be able to determine which specific schools, departments, or projects are candidates for your products and services. Following are some examples of areas you will want to explore and the information/understanding you will gain:

❏ The purchasing/procurement Web pages will likely provide:

　　■ Staff contact information and the guidelines for interacting with them (that is, "You must submit all questions by e-mail")

- Levels and rules of competition (that is, procurements of more than $25,000 must be done by sealed bid)
- Evaluation guidelines
- Payment terms
- Opportunities—invitation for bids, request for proposals, and so on—provide information on the current needs and buying trends and immediate opportunities

❐ If the district is large enough and committed enough, they may have a designated person(s) to aid woman/minority businesses. This person(s) will probably be part of the purchasing/procurement department and will likely have other responsibilities too. If there is a designated person(s) then take advantage of this resource. They can provide information on:

- Projects or departments that are seeking minority vendors
- Special programs, events, and opportunities
- Reports on the goals and the actual dollars spent.
- Changes in policies, goals, programs, and so on.
- "How to do business with" guidance and training notices

A suggested general process for conducting research to identify valid school district government targets for your business is provided in the following pages.

Process for Gathering and Analyzing Information on Public K–12 Education Prospects

Question	Next Step	Tips/Notes
What school districts are in the geographical area I can cover?	Once you have identified the entities move on to the next question.	
Do any of the districts not have a need for my products or services?	If yes, mark then off the list then move on to the next question— Going District by District.	
Does the district have a published policy on the use of woman-owned businesses or W/MBEs?	If yes, move on to the next step. If no, determine if there is a state law that applies.	Remember that you can be the hero by helping them meet a goal or requirement that they haven't had time to even think about.
Does the district have a specified goal for the amount of money to spend with woman-owned businesses?	If yes, move on to the next question. If they have a goal for the use of minority-owned businesses that includes woman owned businesses; continue on to the next step. If the district does not have any goals for woman- or minority-owned business use, then either consider a different approach or plow ahead because you know they are required to encourage W/MBE use.	Remember that you can be the hero by helping them meet a goal or requirement that they haven't had time to even think about.

Question	Next Step	Tips/Notes
Does the district have current projects related to my products/services?	If yes, move on to the next step. If no, research further to determine the buying trends and plans.	Use the information in this chapter on page 137 to find the current opportunities.
Does the district have a designated person to work with woman-owned businesses (or minority businesses, or even small businesses?)	Make note, this is an important qualifying and prioritizing fact.	
Does the district have a history of awarding contracts to woman-owned businesses?	Make note, this is an important qualifying and prioritizing fact.	Use the information in this chapter on pages 134 to research the appropriate Websites.
Are opportunities with the district more likely direct with my company or are they more likely subcontracting opportunities?	If the opportunities are more likely direct, move to the next question. If the opportunities are more likely subcontracting, skip to the analysis process for subcontracting.	Identifying and qualifying subcontracting opportunities are covered in the second part of this chapter beginning on page 140.

Question	Next Step	Tips/Notes
After gathering information on five to 10 districts within a valid target area analyze and rank them according to the previous questions.	This should be your first list of prospects to contact for selling direct. Once you have made initial contact to each of these you will be in the next phase of marketing with them. At that point, you should restart the identification and qualification process with new potential prospects within an area. At the same time you should be looking at additional areas so you can expand your research.	Remember that in an effective marketing plan you will always have several prospects in each phase. We are only covering the initial phase in this chapter. Additional guidance is provided on marketing strategy in Chapter 12.

Subcontracting

Public K–12 education presents the same two opportunities as state and local government, the entity itself and the prime contractors of that entity. However, just as is the case with local government, prime contractors are not always clearly identified for school districts.

Some school districts do have programs/efforts to promote the use of woman- and minority-owned businesses as subcontractors by prime contractors depending on the policy, philosophy, and implementation of the district. Many school districts have a contract requirement/condition that prime contractors use or make a "good faith effort" to use minority subcontractors. Some school districts have established guidelines and measurements for what constitutes a "good faith effort." This type of contract requirement is almost always present in construction for a school district of medium and large size and often the case for small districts; but it is still fairly rare for any product or service not related to construction. The prime contractor is usually required to do one or both of the following:

- ❑ Submit a minority business utilization or subcontracting plan.
- ❑ Show proof of contracts or attempts to obtain minority subcontractors.

A school district may not have some type of program to promote the use of minority subcontractors, but that does not mean that there are no subcontracting opportunities.

Often, small businesses (especially woman- and minority-owned) do not win a bid or get a contract because they cannot meet all the requirements of the project. However, if you are willing to subcontract or partner with other businesses you can dramatically increase your opportunities. This means that you must use a research approach that looks at every opportunity to see if there is a "piece" for you. It also means that you will need to pay attention to the companies that have contracts with school districts to determine if you could "help" them.

Once you have determined that a district is a good target for your business, you want to move on to identify prime contractors and determine which ones are true prospects.

Information on school district prime contractors can be found in the following places:

- ❑ Existing contracts with a district identify businesses that do get contracts with school districts. These contracts are rarely listed on a Website, but are public information. The best approach is usually to tell the purchasing staffer that you are looking for subcontracting opportunities and would like to know who has their contract for the particular product or service you can complement.

There may not be an opportunity for you to subcontract on an existing contract, but it is worth
your time to contact that prime contractor and
let them know about your company for future
contracts with other districts.

☐ Contract awards are another source of information about prime contractors. Some districts post
contract awards on their Websites. Even if they
do not post them, the district usually does provide notice to bidders of contract awards. If you
bid on a project you will know who won the contract. If you do not bid, you can still find out because it is public information. These prime
contractors are potential for current or future
subcontracting opportunities. You will have to
monitor the postings of opportunities and identify those for which you can provide a portion of
the products or services then determine the contract recipient in order to apply this research
method.

☐ Go through at least part of the process of bidding or submitting a proposal. This will provide
you an opportunity to find out what businesses
are interested in the opportunity. One or more
of these may present a subcontracting or
partnering prospect for you. The steps within the
bidding/proposal process that offer a chance to
identify a potential prime contractor prospect are:

  ■ Sometimes the process requires a
    "statement of intent to bid" so that
    addendums to the original request for
    bid/proposal can be sent. Sometimes
    the addendums will include a list of
    potential bidders/proposers.

- For larger projects there is usually a pre-bid meeting/conference—this is an excellent opportunity to actually meet prospective prime contractors. It is worth attending these meetings; even if you do not intend to bid/propose, it is still a great chance to identify and qualify subcontracting prospects.

- A request for bid/proposal may allow vendors to submit questions. You should participate in this even if you do not intend to propose because this will allow you to see the questions (usually identified by vendor) and the answers. This is great information to use in your identification and qualifying efforts. A vendor may expose their subcontracting needs in the questions they ask (that is, "Does the successful bidder have to do the whole project?")

☐ Newspaper announcements about contract awards. These will normally be in the business section because the press release is submitted by the business that won the contract.

All prime contractors will not be a good prospect for you. You will need to do additional research to determine which ones are appropriate. Some of the things that will keep them from being a good prospect for you are:

☐ They can do everything in the contract themselves.

☐ They already have a partnership/subcontracting arrangement with another company. (This does not mean you should cross them completely off your list, they may be a prospect later).

❐ They may have a subsidiary or sister company that does what you do.

❐ They may have a bad reputation for the way they treat subcontractors (be sure you find out the whole story before you cross them off your list).

❐ They may not really be qualified to bid/propose.

The following table provides a suggested process to determine if prime contractors are viable prospects.

Note: You should be evaluating and contacting prospects for direct and subcontracting simultaneously. It often happens that when you are researching or prospecting for one track you find an opportunity in a different track.

Process for Gathering and Analyzing Information on Public K–12 Education Subcontracting

Question	Next Step	Tips/Notes
Guide for Finding Prime Contractors With Existing Contracts		
Does the school district have existing contracts that involve my products/services?	If yes, move on to the next question.	There are tips in this chapter about where and how to find the existing contracts.
Who is the prime contractor on the existing contract that involves my products/services?	Move on to the next question.	
Is this prime contractor capable of meeting all contract requirements alone?	If yes, move the contractor to the bottom of your list. If no, move on to next question.	

Question	Next Step	Tips/Notes
Does this prime contractor already have a subcontractor that provides the same products/services as you?	If yes, still consider contacting the prime contractor, but understand that this is a long-term possibility. If you do contact them, find out how strong the relationship and contract with the current subcontractor is. If no, move on to next step.	
Will this prime contractor benefit from using a woman-owned business (or minority-owned business if that classification includes women)?	If no, consider a different marketing angle to use if you want to pursue being a subcontractor to this prime contractor. If yes, contact them.	This chapter covers possible benefits.
Is this prime contractor likely to bid on similar projects with other districts?	If no, and you do not fit into this specific contract, mark them off your list. If yes, then contact them about future opportunities.	

Guide for Finding Prime Contractors Through the Bidding Process on School District Contracts		
Question	Next Step	Tips/Notes
Is there a bidding or RFP opportunity that involves my products/ services?	If yes, move on to the next question.	Tips on finding opportunities are covered in this chapter on page 137.
Is there a way to find out who the potential bidders or proposing vendors are?	If yes, move on to the next question.	Tips on obtaining this information are provided in this chapter on page 142.
Are the bidders or proposing vendors capable of meeting all the contract/project requirements?	If no, move on to the next question. If yes, move them to the bottom of your list and consider contacting them for future subcontracting opportunities.	
Does this prime contractor already have a subcontractor that provides the same products/services as you?	If no, move on to the next question. If yes, still consider contacting the prime contractor, but understand that this is a long-term possibility. If you do contact them, find out how strong the relationship and contract with the current subcontractor is.	

Question	Next Step	Tips/Notes
Would the bidder or proposing vendor benefit from using a woman-owned business as a subcontractor?	If yes, they are likely a target for you. If no, consider contacting them using a different marketing angle than Woman Owned.	This chapter covers possible benefits on page 141.
Are you familiar enough with the bidder or proposing vendor to know if they would be a good partner?	If yes, contact. If no, do additional research before contacting them.	Good sources for additional information include: the company's Website and the pre-bid meeting.
Is this prime contractor likely to bid on similar projects with other districts?	If no and you do not fit into this specific contract mark them off your list. If yes, then contact them about future opportunities.	

The following questions are designed to help you evaluate the potential prospect and do not necessarily build on each other.

Question	Next Step	Tips/Notes
Does the prime contractor/bidder/proposing vendor have a history of subcontracting with woman-owned businesses?	If yes, enhances your chances.	Remember that this book is about capitalizing on being woman-owned, not fighting causes. If convenience or something similar is the reason there is no history of using woman-owned businesses this may still be a valid prospect.

Question	Next Step	Tips/Notes
Is the school district involved in the bidding/RFP project struggling to meet their goal for the use of woman-owned businesses?	If yes, enhances your chances.	The office/department responsible for implementing the district's minority business Policy normally publishes reports. Other advice on answering this question is provided in this chapter.
Are there other qualified woman-owned businesses registered in the area able to provide the same products/services as you?	If not, your chances increase.	Remember that a business must be certified by the state (or other entity they accept) in order to meet the subcontracting requirements.
Does the prime contractor/bidder/proposing vendor have a designated diversity contact (small business liaison, minority bus developer, and so on) or is the listed contact more general in nature (purchaser, project manager, and so on).	This does not necessarily increase or decrease your chances, but it does provide you some insight for your dealings with the prospect.	You will probably have to investigate the company to find this answer.

Chapter 10

Identifying and Qualifying Prospects:

BUSINESS

More and more businesses are making a serious commitment to ensuring that woman- and minority-owned businesses have equal access to opportunities. Businesses are establishing Policies and setting goals for the use of woman- and minority-owned businesses. Many businesses are also participating in community, statewide and national efforts to support, educate, and prepare woman- and minority-owned businesses.

Businesses usually call their efforts supplier or vendor diversity plans. The majority of businesses use one of these terms—minority-owned business (MOB) or minority business enterprise (MBE). Most businesses include women in this classification. Some use the inclusive acronym W/MBE.

The opportunities for you to sell your products and services to businesses may be directly for their use or they may be to that business for use on a government project, thus making you a subcontractor.

This chapter provides some guidance on identifying and qualifying businesses that may be good prospects for you.

Initial Step

There are directions in Chapter 3 on narrowing your research by identifying the type of business, selecting a geographic area, and choosing the product/service you will market. It is very important to do this narrowing so that your time is spent effectively. This process also reduces the risk that you will give up due to frustration from tackling a research effort that is too large to manage. Not conducting research puts you in jeopardy of just plain wasting your time and possibly damaging your chances by unsuccessfully using your woman-owned status in the wrong places or at the wrong time.

Unlike with government prospects, there are not as many resources to aid in identifying businesses that have supplier/vendor diversity plans. Therefore, you will have to conduct much of the research on your own.

The best place to start is close to home. As pointed out in earlier chapters, starting nearby allows you to take advantage of familiarity with companies, people, and the business climate. Once you have gone through the process of identifying and qualifying local businesses you can move on to other areas in an efficient manner based on what you have learned. Starting in your community with local plants or offices of businesses headquartered elsewhere affords you an opportunity to deal with people you know (or at least know of) in a "warm" situation, instead of a "cold calling" scenario where you call on the business's headquarters. If you are successful with the local presence, then you will increase your chances of selling to the company in other locations.

Policy

There is an overused term employed by sales and marketing folks: *low-hanging fruit*. The term refers to the sales that are within easy reach, just waiting to be plucked. This term is a favorite of sales managers when describing how easy it should be for his/her staff to reach their quotas. After more than 30 years of sales and marketing experience I am still looking for some *low hanging fruit*. The point is that all sales take effort. Printing business cards, setting up a Website, and joining a local business organization are not going to bring in very much business. However, there are prospects that will be easier to turn into customers than others. For a woman-owned business the likeliest prospects are the ones that have a supplier/vendor diversity program.

The policy is the official statement about how the business will recruit, purchase from, and provide support to woman and minority vendors.

Some of the following key phrases and words will be found in the supplier/vendor diversity policies of businesses:

- ❐ We offer woman (minority) businesses opportunity to compete on a par with all other businesses.
- ❐ We promote/encourage the use of woman/minority-owned businesses.
- ❐ We have a supplier diversity liaison/manager.
- ❐ We have a goal of X percent for purchasing dollars spent with woman/minority-owned businesses.
- ❐ We measure purchasing dollars spent with woman/minority-owned businesses.
- ❐ We monitor the effectiveness of our supplier diversity program.
- ❐ Woman/minority-owned businesses are essential to our success.
- ❐ We encourage (or require) our Tier I suppliers to establish supplier diversity policies/plans.

Philosophy

The philosophy of a business is reflected in the policy and is demonstrated by the implementation of that policy. Listed below are some indicators of philosophy:

☐ There is a person (or persons) whose job includes (or is solely) the implementation of the policy.

☐ The business participates in organizations that focus on woman/minority-owned business support and use.

☐ The business sponsors and/or participates in events that are designed to support woman/minority-owned businesses (that is, minority trade fairs, training for W/MBEs, and so on).

☐ The business has won awards for the support and use of woman/minority-owned businesses.

☐ The business has specific measurements for the success of their supplier diversity program.

☐ The business "puts its money where its mouth is." They publish the amount they spend with W/MBE.

Direct Selling

Once you have identified what types of businesses can use your products/services you must then determine which ones have a supplier/vendor diversity program. Here are some places and ways to make that determination.

☐ A business's Website is the first and best place to find the supplier/vendor diversity program. This is where they will provide information on their policy, staff (normally if they have a program there will be at least one person dedicated to it), and associated forms.

- ❏ Participant lists from organizations that support the use and development of woman- and/or minority-owned businesses (that is, sponsors of W/MBE events, funders of a women's business center).

- ❏ Local SBDCs (Small Business Development Center) sometimes maintain lists of businesses with supplier/vendor diversity programs.

- ❏ Local and state offices/departments for the support and development of woman/minority-owned or small businesses sometimes maintain lists of businesses with supplier/vendor diversity programs.

- ❏ Supplier/vendor lists of large companies that have supplier/vendor diversity programs—the supply chain.

- ❏ Local chambers may have knowledge of businesses that have a commitment to the use and support of woman-owned business. This is more likely if the chamber itself has some type of program. Sometimes a chamber will feel that they have done enough if they have a special group for women business owners or conduct a few seminars/networking events for WOBs. (If you are a member of a local chamber you may be able to push them to do more in the support of WOBs including maintaining a list of businesses committed to the use and support.)

- ❏ Local news media may publish news about businesses that have received some type of award associated with the use/support of woman- and minority-owned businesses. This information is usually in the business section.

❐ Other woman- or minority-owned businesses may be willing to trade information on good prospects with you.

❐ A call to the business is a last resort method, but can be used if done properly. If you cannot find out any other way, you can make a call to the purchasing/procurement department or person and ask for information on becoming a vendor to them. If they have a published policy or guide, ask for a copy. If they do not have anything published ask them about the procedure to register as a vendor. During the conversation you can ask if they have any special programs or policies that deal with small businesses, woman/minority-owned businesses or disadvantaged businesses. This method will not only allow you to understand what it takes to be a vendor to this business, it will also facilitate the answer to your question about a diversity program without being aggressive about it.

Note: It is important to remember that purchasing/ procurement staff are extremely careful about committing to anything; they sometimes are concerned that an affirmation of a policy may be seen as a commitment. Also, if you lead with the diversity question you may be seen as having a sense of entitlement, which can be a strong negative.

Following is a table to aid you in identifying and qualifying business prospects.

Process for Gathering and Analyzing Information on Business Prospects

Question	Next Step	Tips/Notes
Does the business have need of my products/services?	If yes, move on to the next question. If no, remove from your list.	
Does the business have a specified goal for the amount of money to spend with woman-owned businesses?	If yes, move on to the next question. If no, move business to the bottom of your list.	If you know the business has immediate need of your products/services, then consider approaching them using a different angle than woman-owned.
Does the business have need for my products/services in my specified geographic area(s)?	If you cannot find this information, then skip to the next question.	
Does the business have a location/site/office in my specified geographic area(s)?	If yes, move on to the next question. If no, move business down your list for reconsideration when your specified geographic area includes the locations/sites/offices of this business.	The business's Website and local telephone directories are two good sources for this information.
Does the business have a designated person to work with woman/minority-owned businesses?	Make note, this is an important qualifying and prioritizing fact.	The business's Website is probably the best place to find this information.

Question	Next Step	Tips/Notes
Does the business ever give preference to woman/minority-owned businesses?	Make note, this is an important qualifying and prioritizing fact.	The business's Website is probably the best place to find this information.
Does the business have a history of awarding contracts to woman-owned businesses?	Make note, this is an important qualifying and prioritizing fact.	The business's Website and your local chamber are possibilities for finding this information
What is this business's philosophy for using woman-owned businesses?	Make note, this is important qualifying and prioritizing information. If they do not have a policy specific to WOBs, look at the overall philosophy for the use of small and minority businesses	The business may have a published policy or plan.
Are opportunities with this business more likely direct between my company and the business or are they more likely subcontracting opportunities?	If the opportunities are more likely direct, move to the next question. If the opportunities are more likely subcontracting, skip to the analysis process for subcontracting.	Identifying and qualifying subcontracting opportunities are covered in the second part of this chapter on page 157.
After gathering information on 10 to 20 businesses analyze and rank according to the previous questions. Don't limit to one type of business, but diversify your research the first few times to determine the best types of business targets.	This should be your first list of prospects to contact for selling direct. Once you have made initial contact to each, you will be in the next phase of marketing. At that point you should restart the identification and qualification process with new potential prospects.	Remember: In an effective marketing plan you will always have several prospects in each phase. We are only covering the initial phase in this chapter. Additional guidance on marketing strategy in Chapter 12.

Subcontracting

Sometimes subcontracting is the best approach for marketing to businesses. This means that your company provides a portion of the products and/or services specified in a contract or project. There are two paths for subcontracting to businesses. One path is providing some products and services of a project/contract to the business through another business which is the prime contractor. The second path is in supplying some products or services on a contract between government and a business. The business in that case is the prime contractor. In either path your contract would be with the prime contractor.

Some of the reasons why this approach may be advantageous for you are:

❐ You might not be equipped or qualified to handle the project alone.

❐ You may not want to attempt the project alone or as the prime contractor because the project is:

◼ Too complex

◼ Too time consuming

◼ Requirements for such things as insurance or bonding are financial obstacles

❐ The business is a prime contractor to a government or education entity and there are advantages for you and the prime contractor in this arrangement. More specific information on subcontracting to government and education is provided in earlier chapters.

❐ The project covers multiple geographic areas and you cannot serve all of them.

❐ You do not have a track record for providing products and services to a specific type of business and want to earn a reputation for capability and quality through being a subcontractor.

If you want to pursue the idea of being a subcontractor on contracts and projects that provide products and services to a business you will need to identify that business's prime contractors. The best place to begin is with the businesses supply chain. This is the chain of vendors that are necessary for the business to do business. The business actually has two supply chains—the one that is directly related to the businesses product/service and the one that is indirect. As stated earlier in this chapter, many large businesses who have supplier diversity policies encourage/require their suppliers to also use W/MBEs. Some of the places you discover the supply chain of a business are:

- ❒ Business's supplier diversity Web page and/or staff
- ❒ Business's reports and publications (annual report, SEC reports, Investor Relations materials)
- ❒ Local chamber or economic development organization
- ❒ Supply chain groups associated with a specific industry/type of business or even a specific business (that is, the automotive industry or a specific auto manufacturer)
- ❒ Professional organizations
- ❒ Organizations focused on support of woman- or minority-owned businesses such as:
  - ■ State or local woman/minority-owned office or department
  - ■ State department of transportation's DBE (Disadvantaged Business Enterprise) Program
  - ■ Women's Business Enterprise National Council (WBENC)

- - National Woman Business Owners Council (NWBOC)
  - National (or regional) Minority Supplier Development Council (NMSDC)
- Media such as:
  - Local newspapers, TV
  - Local business publications
  - Trade/professional publications
- State department of commerce (sometimes a large company's suppliers are receiving tax incentives and the DOC will have records).

The second path of subcontracting to businesses is on government and education projects. There are some generalities, but more specifics for being a subcontractor for the various government and education entities. Listed below are the assorted entities and the chapter that provides details on prospect identification and qualification of each of them:

- Chapter 4—Federal Government
- Chapter 5—State Government
- Chapter 6—Local Government
- Chapter 7—State Supported Education
- Chapter 8—Private Education
- Chapter 9—Public K–12 Schools

A few major points for this type of subcontracting are:

- Subcontractors on federal government contracts must be registered with the CCR (Central Contractor Registration) *www.ccr.gov*. CCR is the database used by the federal government and its prime contractors to identify potential vendors/suppliers.

☐ Many government and education entities require prime contractors to use W/MBEs as subcontractors on some projects or show proof that they tried.

☐ SBA provides a list of prime contractors located in each state that offer subcontracting opportunities. The prime contractor is listed by the state in which they are headquartered; however, they may need subcontractors in other states, depending on the requirements of their contract(s) with the federal government. Contact information is provided. The Website is *www.sba.gov/GC/indexcontacts-sbsd.html*.

The following table provides a suggested process to identify and evaluate prime contractors that are providing products and services to a business. Processes for subcontracting on government and education entities are detailed in individual chapters as listed earlier in this chapter.

Process to Identify and Evaluate Prime Contractors

Question	Next Step	Tips/Notes
Are the opportunities with a specific business better handled in a subcontracting arrangement?	If yes, move on to next question. If no, refer back to direct process	
Is a prime contractor working or bidding on projects for which my products/services are appropriate?	If yes, move on to the next question. If no, reevaluate direct opportunities.	

Question	Next Step	Tips/Notes
Does the prime contractor have a contract or is bidding on a project that needs my products/services in a geographic area I can serve?	If yes, move on to the next question. If no, reevaluate prime contractor in the future for match of geographic area.	
Does the prime contractor already have their subcontracting plan?	If no, contact immediately. If yes, move on to the next question.	
If there are no opportunities on a current contract, is it likely the prime contractor will bid on future projects for which my products or services and geographic area are appropriate?	If no, move to the bottom of your list for future contact. If yes, move on to the next question.	
Does the prime contractor have a history of subcontracting with w o m a n - o w n e d businesses?	If yes, move on to the next question. If no, try to determine why and decide whether or not to pursue.	Remember that this book is about capitalizing on being woman-owned, not fighting causes. If convenience or something similar is the reason there is no history of using woman-owned businesses this may still be a valid prospect.

Question	Next Step	Tips/Notes
The following questions are designed to help you evaluate the potential prospect and do not necessarily build on each other.		
Is the business involved in the project or bid struggling to meet their goal or contract requirement for the use of woman-owned businesses?	If yes, enhances your chances.	
Are there other qualified woman-owned businesses that can provide substantial competition?	If not, your chances increase.	
Does the prime contractor have a designated diversity contact (small business liaison, minority bus developer, and so on) or is the listed contact more general in nature (purchaser, project manager, and so on)?	This does not necessarily increase or decrease your chances, but it does provide you some insight for your dealings with the prospect.	
After gathering information on eight to 10 prime contractors analyze and rank them according to the previous questions.	This should be your first list of prospects to contact for subcontracting. Once you have made initial contact, you will be in the next phase of marketing with them. At that point you should begin the identification and qualification process over with new potential prospects.	Remember that in an effective marketing plan you will always have several prospects in each phase. We are only covering the initial phase in this chapter.

Note: You should be evaluating and contacting prospects for direct and subcontracting simultaneously. It often happens that when you are researching or prospecting for one track you find an opportunity in a different track.

Chapter 11

Should My Business Be Certified?

TYPES AND BENEFITS OF CERTIFICATION

Certification as a woman-owned business (or other applicable classification) is an advantageous, and often required, designation for capitalizing on being woman owned. There are many certifications that can be of benefit. Each certification has its own requirements and process; however, there are many similarities. This chapter provides information to help you understand the types of certifications and how they can benefit you.

Before the types of certifications are discussed, there are a few factors that you need to know:

❑ Being certified is not an end, it is step in maximizing your woman owned status. Many women business-owners assume that once they are on a list of certified businesses, the customers will start calling. The reality is that you must let prospects know that you exist and are certified. More information on how to do this is provided in Chapter 12.

❑ Even if you are certified, you may also have to "register" with a prospect to actually be on the list that purchasers use to find vendors. Some examples of registrations are provided in Chapter 12.

❐ Some certifying entities will automatically certify you if you already have other specific certifications. More detail is provided later in this chapter; however, here is an example: *A county office of minority affairs may automatically certify you, if you are already certified by the home state of that county. Therefore, you would want to obtain the state level certification first.* It is important to investigate these reciprocal certifications because it could expand your prospects and/or save you a lot of time and effort.

❐ Certifications are always based on ownership and require that a business be at least 51-percent owned by the appropriate classification of person for the certification (that is, if the certification is for a woman-owned business then it must be at least 51-percent owned by a woman or women). There is usually a requirement that the business also be managed by a woman. This means that the owner must be involved in the business operation and is evidenced by such things as:

- She negotiates the contracts
- She approves major purchases
- She signs the checks (or has oversight of signing)
- She has the necessary licenses, degrees, certifications, etc. to perform the functions of the business (that is, if it's an architectural firm, she has an architectural license)

❐ Most certification processes include a site visit to your place of business. Home offices are normally acceptable as a place of business as long as there is a definant space that is set aside for your work area and is suitable for the type of business you own.

❏ Almost all certifications that apply to woman-owned businesses require that the certified individual be a U.S. citizen; however, some do accept U.S. resident alien status.

❏ Ownership by your company in other related businesses and by other companies in your business are evaluated by many certifying entities in determining whether you will be certified. Bear in mind that one of the primary purposes of certifications is to help insure that all businesses have an equal opportunity and certain affiliations may be considered detrimental to that effort.

❏ Many certifications are designed to aid businesses that are in need; therefore, your financial situation can be a qualifier. There is usually a "net worth" limit for a business applying to be certified. Business and personal tax filings and financial statements are required.

❏ Purchasers use certification credentials as a means of ensuring that they are using businesses that are actually woman owned. This is a way of screening out businesses that may be a "front" for another business that is not woman-owned. Certifications that have a net worth limitation will not be renewed when the owner exceeds the limit. It is the viewpoint of the certifying entities that the program has done its job and the business has "graduated."

Each type of certification has its own benefits and is accepted/required/preferred by different businesses and government or education entities. It is very important that you follow the process detailed in earlier chapters to identify your prospects before deciding which certification is best for you. A general guide is provided at the end of this chapter to help you in your decision.

Federal Certifications

There are no federal government certifications for woman-owned businesses. However, there are some certifications that benefit WOBs. All applicable federal certifications are handled by the Small Business Administration (SBA).

There are three core certification programs offered by the SBA. Details on qualifying, applying for, and benefiting from the SBA certifications can be found at: *www.sba.gov/ training/certprograms.html#The*. Also, most SBA regional offices provide orientation sessions on qualifying and applying for these certifications.

SDB (Small Disadvantaged Business)

This program is intended to bring about equality of opportunity for small businesses whose circumstances put them at a disadvantage. An applying business must show that it is socially disadvantaged. The social disadvantage must be beyond the control of the applying business. One of the evidences used for qualification is gender; however, being woman-owned does not automatically qualify a business for SDB certification. Because this is a certification that is designed to help small businesses in need the net worth of the individual claiming disadvantage (the business owner) must be less than $750,000 (less exclusions allowed by law).

The SDB certification provides two benefits:

❐ Qualification for a price evaluation adjustment if the certified business bids on a federal government project as the prime contractor.

❐ Advantage in being chosen as a subcontractor by the prime contractor on federal government projects. (See Chapter 4 for more details about subcontracting on federal government projects.)

If you want to sell your products/services to the federal government, either directly or by subcontracting, this certification will provide you definite advantages. Some projects are set aside for SDB certified businesses. Also, many projects require prime contractors to use as subcontractors small businesses certified by the SBA under one of its three core programs.

SDB is the program for which most woman-owned businesses are likely to qualify.

8(a) Business Development Program

Helping small disadvantaged businesses compete is the objective of this program. It is a nine-year program and actually has two stages: developmental and transitional. In the developmental stage, the certified business receives help in overcoming their economic disadvantage through personalized counseling. In the transitional stage, the business is paired with a business opportunity specialist for coaching on growing and expanding its business.

A business certified as 8(a) is automatically considered a SDB and entitled to all benefits of that program.

This program is based primarily on financial situation so the following requirements apply:

❐ For initial eligibility the net worth of the individual claiming disadvantage (the business owner) must be less than $250,000 (less certain exclusions allowed by law).

❏ For continued eligibility (through the entire nine years of the program) the net worth must be less than $750,000 (minus certain exclusions allowed by law).

This program is advantageous if you want to sell your products/services to the federal government, either directly or by subcontracting. If you are certified as 8(a) you qualify for the projects that are set aside specifically for 8(a) certified businesses and for those that are set aside for SDB. Also, many projects require prime contractors to use as subcontractors small businesses certified by the SBA under one of its three core programs.

Note: Many prime contractors are seeking subcontractors that are 8(a) or SDB certified. They usually specify that they need 8(a) subcontractors even when SDB is sufficient. If you have a SDB certification you may have to use the regional SBA office or the OSDBU (Office of Small Disadvantaged Business Utilization) of the purchasing federal agency or department to aid the prime contractor in understanding that you can help them meet their subcontracting requirements. (More information on SBA and OSDBU offices is provided in Chapter 4).

The title of this certification, 8(a), is taken from the paragraph number of the law that established the small disadvantage business program.

HUBZone Empowerment Contracting Program

The goal of this program is to encourage economic development and produce jobs in urban and rural communities. In order to qualify for this program you must be located in an area that has already been designated as a HUB (HUB = Historically Underutilized Business) Zone. The SBA Regional Office can assist you in determining if you are located in a HUB Zone.

This program does have contracts set aside for businesses that qualify.

Most state and local government entities will recognize either of these certifications by the small business administration. You may still want to obtain a certification from a state or local government entity, but the process should be greatly simplified.

National Certifications

Even though there is no federal certification for woman-owned businesses, there are two private entities that do certify businesses as being woman owned—Women's Business Enterprise National Council (WBENC) and the National Women Business Owners Corporation (NWBOC). These certifications are based simply on ownership and management. A qualifying firm must be at least 51-percent owned by a woman or women. There must also be proof that the woman owner is involved in the day-to-day operation and management of the business, not an absentee owner.

Each of the organizations has their own application and certification process. The process does require financial information similar to that required by the SBA and state and local government entities. The financial information is primarily required in order to determine that the applying WOB is a valid business, financially sound, and capable of meeting its customer/client needs. There is a charge.

The Websites for these certifying organizations are:
WBENC: *www.wbenc.org/certification/index.html*
NWBOC: *www.nwboc.org/certific.html*

These certifications are recognized by many businesses. They provide significant competitive advantages with businesses that have a supplier/vendor diversity policy. More information on identifying these prospects is provided in Chapter 10. Some government and education entities, especially federal, also recognize or accept these certifications. When determining if one of these certifications would be of benefit, you should:

❑ Decide if you want to do business outside your state

❑ Determine if you have any national prospects that need more than a local or state certification

❑ Determine that you do *not* qualify under the financial requirements for other certifications based partially on need

If the answer to all of these is no, you may not need to consider one of these national certifications.

There is a nationwide certification provided by the National Minority Supplier Development Council (NMSDC) for minority-owned businesses. Women are not considered a minority by this organization. A business owner must be part of one of the groups recognized by the organization as a minority. This certification is recognized by many of the same businesses that accept the woman-owned business certification from WBENC and NWBOC. If you qualify for certification as a minority-owned business you may want to explore certification by the NMSDC before pursuing it with WBENC or NWBOC. It is a membership organization. There are local chapters of all three of these organizations/affiliations in some areas of the country. You should evaluate the other benefits or these organizations and determine which ones apply to you and which ones you can easily take advantage of before choosing a certification.

State Certifications

General

Most states offer a certification for woman- and/or minority-owned businesses. The majority of states offer a minority-owned business certification that recognizes women as a minority. A few states do not include woman-owned businesses in their certifications for minority-owned businesses. Because this type of policy is very tied to the political climate and therefore subject to change, this book does not attempt to provide any specific details. This chapter does provide information and guidance on conducting research to determine the policy of a state.

Many states create an office or department to implement its policy for the use and support of minority businesses. That office or department normally manages the certification process for the state as outlined in the procurement or purchasing laws/codes. This office or department is typically part of the governor's office, the department of commerce, or the procurement/purchasing department.

The certification normally has a name that includes the word "certification" and one or more of the following:

- ❒ Minority- and/or woman-owned business
- ❒ Minority and/or woman business enterprise (MBE or W/MBE)
- ❒ Underutilized business or historically underutilized business (HUB)

When doing research in a state that you have determined is a good target, start your hunt for certification information by using the previouslu mentioned terms through the state's

Website search engine. If that is not successful or the state's Website does not have a search engine, look at the procurement/purchasing Web page. Other possibilities are the governor's office and the department of commerce. If you cannot find information on the Website you can:

❐ Ask the procurement/purchasing department/ office

❐ Ask the governor's office

❐ Ask the regional SBA (Small Business Administration) office or SBDC (Small Business Development center)

❐ Ask the department of commerce small business department or person

The customary requirements by a state for certification are:

❐ 51 percent ownership by a woman or women

❐ Owner is involved in day-to-day operation

❐ Owner has appropriate credentials, license, certificates, and so on

❐ Owner(s) is a U.S. citizen

❐ Business has a location within the certifying state (common but not required by all)

❐ Individual (owner) has a net worth of $750,000 or less (often allows for exclusion of residence in the net worth calculation)

Most states require that woman and minority businesses be certified in order to qualify for use by the state and its prime contractors in meeting the set goals. Some states only accept their own certification in these situations. Therefore, if you have determined that a specific state government is a good prospect for your business, you definantly need to understand the state's specific requirements. Certification is not a requirement for doing business with the agencies, departments, and institutions of a state, but can provide you a competitive plus.

Department of Transportation (DOT)

The Department of Transportation (DOT) in the majority of States offers a certification that is applicable to woman-owned businesses. DOTs certify businesses as being a Disadvantaged Business Enterprise (DBE). Owner gender is one of the factors that help qualify a business as a DBE.

This certification follows federal guidelines similar to those for SDB (see information in previous section in this chapter on federal certifications) because DOTs receive federal funding. The DOTs normally have an office that works with DBEs to ensure they have an equal opportunity in competing for contracts. In addition to processing the certification applications they may also:

❑ Provide training and guidance on such things as marketing, bid preparation, and computer use.

❑ Maintain a database of certified businesses for use by DOT departments, project managers, and prime contractors.

❑ Conduct matchmaking sessions for DBEs with DOT purchasers and prime contractors.

❑ Conduct mentoring initiatives.

DOTs used to concentrate their efforts to assist DBEs on construction projects, but most have expanded to include all products and services used. When you are identifying and qualifying prospects you should evaluate state DOTs because the scope of their needs are wide and may very well include your products/services. In your evaluation you should determine the certification requirements. As with any state entity you are not required to be certified in order to do business with them, but it does provide a competitive advantage.

Each state's DOT does its own certifications; however, some have reciprocal agreements with other state DOTs. It is important to discover any such agreements to be sure you take advantage of them and not duplicate your certification efforts in individual states.

Some states have combined all their certifications under one umbrella. This collective certification may use the disadvantaged business enterprise name or may have been renamed combined certification.

Even if a state has a general certification for woman- or minority-owned businesses they may accept or honor their DOTs certification for DBE. However, the state DOTs do not normally accept the state certification. This is primarily because the DOT must strictly follow national guidelines and states may use their own requirements and parameters.

Local Certifications

Municipalities, counties, and even school districts sometimes offer their own certifications for woman- and minority-owned businesses. In the past this typically occurred in a state that did not have a statewide certification. However, local certification is becoming more common. Local government entities have recognized the fact that if the woman and minority-owned businesses are successful the overall economy benefits and the tax base is increased. The local governments feel that certification is a key part of a development program for woman/minority-owned businesses or small businesses. This allows them to establish parameters that compliment their development program and validate that a business qualifies. The requirements are usually similar to those for state certifications. They may not include the net worth limit as a condition.

Local government and education certifications are normally handled by one of the following:

- ❑ Office/department of minority affairs
- ❑ Women/minority business development program or office
- ❑ Small business development program or office
- ❑ Procurement or purchasing office or department

Very often, local governments that have a certification program will honor other certifications such as:

- ❑ Statewide
- ❑ Department of Transportation's Disadvantaged Business Enterprise
- ❑ Any of the three core U.S. Small Business Administration (SBA) certifications
- ❑ Women's Business Enterprise National Council (WBENC)
- ❑ National Women Business Owners Corporation (NWBOC)
- ❑ Other local certifications

In order to determine if a local certification is advisable, you must conduct research on your target prospects. The Website of a local government or education entity is the best place to start. If you cannot find the information on the Website and you do not see evidence of a development program for woman/minority-owned businesses, you can ask the procurement/purchasing staff.

Other Benefits and Advice

Certifications can provide one or more of the following benefits:

- ❏ Qualification for specific loans or for higher loan amounts.
- ❏ Advantage for participating in development grants.
- ❏ Qualification for participating in a development program for woman/minority-owned businesses.
- ❏ Qualification for participating in women's business center activities and assistance.

As you can see, there are many choices of certifications and each has its own set of requirements and benefits. This makes it very important that you develop your list of prospects and your marketing plan before you make a decision about which certifications best apply to your business. This formula gives you an idea of the possible number of available certifications:

General in each state	50
DOT's DBE in each state	50
Conservative estimate of 5 local in each state	250
SBA [8(a), SDB, HUBZone]	3
+ Private (WBENC, NWBOC, NMSDC)	3
Total	356

Following is a suggested process to aid you in your evaluation.

Important note: Do not make an assumption about which certification is best! It is vital that you do the research to determine which one is accepted/required by your prospect. The following table is a guide to assist you; it is not a finite formula. Also, if you have prospects of several different types it is important that you determine the reciprocal/complimentary conditions of all possible certifications so that you do not have to go through any more application systems than is absolutely necessary. Don't give up because it is complicated; if you do the research and map out a plan the complication, time, and effort will be lessened.

Process for Evaluating Certifications

You Want to Sell Your Products or Services to:	Probable Type of Certification	Also Consider
Municipalities and counties	Local government certifications if they exist, if not the certification for the home state of the municipality or county	>State's DOT DBE >SBA 8(a) or SDB >WBENC or NWBOC *(Be sure that your prospect accepts a certification before you do the work involved in an application)*
School districts	The school district's certification if it exists, if not the certification for the home state of the school district or a local certification if it exists	>State's DOT DBE >SBA 8(a) or SDB >WBENC or NWBOC *(Be sure that your prospect accepts a certification before you do the work involved in an application)*
Prime contractor to municipality, county, or school district	Local certification if it exists, if not the certification for the home state of the municipality, county, or school district	>State's DOT DBE >SBA 8(a) or SDB >WBENC or NWBOC *(Be sure that the customer/client of the prime contractor accepts a certification before you do the work involved in an application)*
State supported education institution (college, university, community or technical college, and so on)	State's woman/minority business certification	>State's DOT DBE >SBA 8(a) or SDB >WBENC or NWBOC *(Be sure that your prospect accepts a certification before you do the work involved in an application)*

You Want to Sell Your Products or Services to:	Probable Type of Certification	Also Consider
State agency, department, or institution (other than DOT)	State's woman/minority business certification	>State's DOT DBE >SBA 8(a) or SDB >WBENC or NWBOC *(Be sure that your prospect accepts a certification before you do the work involved in an application)*
Prime contractor for state agency, department, institution, or education facility (other than DOT)	State's woman/minority business certification	>State's DOT DBE >SBA 8(a) or SDB >WBENC or NWBOC *(Be sure that your prospect accepts a certification before you do the work involved in an application)*
A state's Department of Transportation (DOT)	DBE certification of the state's DOT	>SBA 8(a) or SDB >WBENC or NWBOC *(Be sure that your prospect accepts a certification before you do the work involved in an application)*
Prime contractor of a state's DOT	DBE certification of the state's DOT	>SBA 8(a) or SDB >WBENC or NWBOC *(Be sure that your prospect accepts a certification before you do the work involved in an application)*

You Want to Sell Your Products or Services to:	Probable Type of Certification	Also Consider
Federal government agency, department, or institution	SBA 8(a), SDB or HUBZone	>WBENC or NWBOC >Your home state's woman/minority business certification >Your home state's DOT DBE certification
Prime contractor of a federal government agency, department, or institution	SBA 8(a), SDB or HUBZone	>WBENC or NWBOC >Your home state's woman/minority business certification >Your home State's DOT DBE Certification *(Sometimes federal prime contractors are limited to the use of subcontractors that are certified by one of the SBA's 3 core programs: 8(a), SDB, or HUBZone)*
Business that has a supplier or vendor diversity policy with headquarters outside your home state	WBENC or NWBOC	>SBA 8(a), SDB, or HUB Zone >State woman/minority certification of the business's home state or your home state. *(Be sure that your prospect accepts a certification before you do the work involved in an application)*

You Want to Sell Your Products or Services to:	Probable Type of Certification	Also Consider
Business that has a supplier or vendor diversity policy with headquarters inside your home state	State woman/minority certification of your homestate	>WBENC or NWBOC *(Be sure that your prospect accepts a certification before you do the work involved in an application)*
Supplier to large corporations that require their vendors to use woman/minority businesses	*The best choice is the certification that is preferred/required by the large corporation*	

Chapter 12

Marketing Strategy:
APPLYING RESEARCH, PUBLICIZING, AND BUILDING SELLING RELATIONSHIPS

Marketing is about angles—knowing the right angle and using it effectively to promote, sell, incite, or cause change. Woman-owned businesses have a built in angle. This chapter presents advice and guidance on using that built in angle effectively.

A marketing strategy or plan normally includes activities to educate prospects. The current buying environment places emphasis on the importance of supplier diversity so you do not have to spend a lot of your time and effort on raising the awareness of this matter. However, many buyers and users still do not understand the benefits of supplier diversity and/or that women are, or should be, included in the minority classification. The guidance in this chapter is designed to assist you in incorporating the specific education and awareness for prospects that will make your efforts more successful.

Introduce Yourself

Obtaining woman-owned certifications takes a lot of time and effort. Agencies and organizations providing certifications stress the fact that once you are certified you will be on a list used by a large number of purchasers. The actuality is that the purchasers do not always, sometimes ever, look at those lists. The old adage that "people buy from people" is still very accurate. Usually one of the following will happen before purchasers *resort* to the list:

- ❒ They will solicit bids/proposals from vendors they have dealt with previously.
- ❒ They will solicit bids/proposals from vendors known by someone they trust (a colleague, a peer, or even a competitor).
- ❒ They will solicit bids/proposals from vendors with whom they are familiar because:
  - ■ They have met them.
  - ■ They have appropriate information from them.
  - ■ They have read about or heard of them.
- ❒ They will solicit bids/proposals from vendors that their company, agency, department, and so on, has done business with in the past.

So even though certifications are a beneficial, sometimes-necessary, first step you cannot expect that the opportunities will start to roll in once you are on a list as being certified. You must make yourself known to the purchasers in order to get the opportunities. You absolutely have to make your company and yourself known to your prospects.

The first step is to introduce your business to prospects. If you have just opened your doors for business and do not have any type of certification you can still let people know that you exist and that you are woman-owned. However, if you claim woman-owned status, most purchasers will ask if you are certified and will want to see the credentials. You may want to save any reference about being woman-owned until you obtain a certification. This will give you a chance to receive additional attention from prospects later on by announcing that you have received a certification.

Once you have obtained a certification you should publicize it by:

❐ Printing it on your business cards.

❐ Including it on your Website. Place it on the first page where the Internet search engines will find it and on at least one other page. If you have more than one certification you might devote a page to certifications and have a link on the first page to the certification page.

❐ Including it on your marketing materials—brochures, flyers, mail outs, and so on.

❐ Sending a press release announcing that your business "has been certified by (fill in appropriate agency/organization)" to:

■ Local daily and weekly newspapers. Usually this type of article will only be printed in an area where you have a presence. If you have a presence (office, sales person, plant, and so on) in a location you can possibly get coverage if you tailor your press release to include the fact that you have an office, sales staff, and so on, in the area of that publication. Below is an example of wording:

Entrepreneur, LLC, a big-city-based company with a sales office in Podunk City, has been certified as a woman-owned business by the state office of minority support.

- Local business publications. The same rules apply here as for daily and weekly newspapers.

- Local chamber for their newsletter (if you are a member).

- Organizations in which you participate for inclusion in their newsletters.

- Existing customers/clients and prospects that you have contacted at least once before. A press release is usually better than an announcement because it seems more official.

❏ Include in any ads you run in any type of media. You will need to evaluate the audience and determine if it should be treated as a major or minor piece of the advertisement. Additional information about understanding when to effectively use WOB status later in this chapter will assist you in making this determination.

❏ Include in your newsletter if you publish one. Treat it as an article or announcement when you first receive a certification. In all subsequent issues include it with the other general information (address, Website, contact information).

❏ Consider including an appropriate phrase on your stationery. Right under your address and phone number you could print something such as "Certified by the X Office of Minority Affairs."

☐ Display the certification credential on the wall in your business, preferably the most public space—reception area, hallway, and so on.

☐ Display your exhibit materials, especially if you are exhibiting at an event that includes prospects that will benefit from your woman-owned status.

☐ Include the certification when you introduce yourself if the venue is appropriate. An example of this: You are attending a marketing workshop and the other participants are potential clients/customers or partners that need woman-owned subcontractors. If they allow participants to introduce themselves be sure you mention your certification(s).

The previous list for publicizing activities is general in nature. You will also need to more directly introduce your company and your certification credentials to your prospects. A great deal of this book concentrates on identifying and qualifying prospects. This is emphasized so that you can be more effective in your marketing and sales efforts. When you know who your prospects are and understand how they can benefit from your woman-owned status you will not only be more effective, you will also save yourself a lot of time, money, and frustration. It is vital that you know enough about your prospects to show them how your business can specifically meet their needs. Many purchasers criticize vendors for not taking the time to understand them, their needs, and their processes. The following actions are designed to build on the identification and qualification research you have done.

Prospects that do certification (that is, federal, state, local governments) will sometimes have more than one list from which they draw bidders/proposers. Obtaining the certification normally places you on the list of certified woman, minority, or disadvantaged businesses. Nevertheless, you may also need to register as a vendor to be placed on the list with all other vendors. As a rule, you have to fill out a form either online or in hard copy—usually called a vendor registration form. Typically this form allows you to note that you are a woman-owned business and state the specific certifications you have attained. This is usually posted, along with the other information about your company, on the vendor list. This vendor list is usually the first place purchasers and users look for businesses to meet their product and service needs. Never assume that being certified by an entity will automatically place you on the vendor list. Being on both the certified list and the vendor list increases your chances.

The crucial first step in marketing is to follow the directions you uncovered in your research. If your prospect has a process—follow it to the letter.

There are both similarities and differences in dealing with business, government, and education entities. The following tables provide guidance through typical processes for making your business known to a prospect in the various classifications covered in this book. The tables specific to a prospect type stand alone so that you can easily use the one that applies to you in any given situation. The suggested actions that are common to all are provided in a separate table.

It is important to follow the sequence outlined here. This process will "grease the gears" because you are following the preferred method and not circumventing any steps or requirements.

Marketing to Federal Government

Situation	Action	Notes
The agency, department, or office requires certification?	Be sure that you have the proper certification.	OSDBU (office of small disadvantaged business utilization) Website and staff are the best sources.
The agency, department, or office requires registration on a vendor list?	Complete the vendor registration form (follow the instructions precisely). Be sure to accurately note your woman-owned status.	There may be separate vendor lists for various divisions within the federal entity. It is important that you do your identification and qualifying research in order to determine which divisions are the best prospects for you. No need to fill out more forms than necessary.
The agency, department, or office catalogs and forwards information on woman, minority, or disadvantaged businesses to divisional purchasers and users?	Provide the appropriate office/staff with information on your business including your certifications.	This function will likely be performed by the OSDBU.
The agency, department, or office has staff assigned to helping them reach their goals for the use of woman-owned businesses?	Contact all appropriate staff and provide them information on your business. There may be a person for the entire agency, department, or office; there may also be staff for the various divisions.	Usually these folks will instruct you to complete the vendor registration form before they will talk with you. That is why this process directs you to complete the form *before* making contact.

Situation	Action	Notes
In your research you identified specific divisions and locations that you want to target.	Contact the purchasing/procurement staff and provide them information on your business and certifications. From the research you did during the identification and qualification process you will know if purchasing is done on a centralized or decentralized basis. You may need to contact a local or divisional purchasing office or person in addition or instead of the main purchasing/procurement office.	Purchasing/procurement offices are rule keepers, they: > Ensure the purchased product or service is of proper quality and reasonably priced. > Ensure vendors are capable and financially sound. > Ensure that all vendors have an equal opportunity. > Ensure that any special requirements or set asides for the use of woman, minority, or disadvantaged business are enforced.
You realize that the purchasing/procurement staff are not the users.	Contact the users of your products or services and tell them about your business and certification.	Begin the conversation or correspondence with a phrase such as this: "We have already registered as a vendor and provided information to the purchasing office, but because we know you are trying to meet your goals for the use of woman-owned businesses we wanted to contact you directly."
Skip to Common Actions table (page 202)		

Marketing to State Government and State-Supported Education

Situation	Action	Notes
The agency, department, office, or institution requires certification?	Be sure that you have the proper certification.	Most states have their own certification, but may accept others. Chapter 11 on certification has additional guidance on this.
The purchasing arm of most states is totally separate from the office/department that does certification and therefore maintains its own database of vendors.	Complete the vendor registration form for each state where you want to do business (follow the instructions precisely). Be sure to accurately note your woman-owned status.	There may be separate vendor lists for various agencies, departments, offices, or institutions within a state. Two examples are: Department of Transportation (DOT) and information/technology services (IT).
The agency, department office, or institution has staff assigned to helping them reach their goals for the use of woman- or minority-owned businesses.	Contact all appropriate staff and provide them information on your business. There may be a person for the entire agency, department, or office; there may also be staff for the various divisions.	Sometimes these folks will instruct you to complete the vendor registration form before they will talk with you. That is why this process directs you to complete the form *before* making contact.

Situation	Action	Notes
In your research you identified agencies, departments, offices, or institutions that you want to target.	Contact the purchasing/procurement staff of those identified and provide them information on your business and certifications. From the research you did during the identification and qualification process you will know the rules governing purchases (that is, all purchases of more than $10,000 must have three bids)	Purchasing/procurement offices are rule keepers, they: > Ensure purchased product or service is of proper quality and reasonably priced. > Ensure vendors are capable and financially sound > Ensure that all vendors have an equal opportunity > Ensure that the state's procurement code is followed.
You realize that the purchasing/procurement staff are not the users.	Contact the users of your products or services and tell them about your business and certification(s).	Sometimes the user is allowed to determine who will receive notification of the bid or proposal request. You will not be on their list if they do know about you. Begin the conversation or correspondence with a phrase such as this: "We have already registered as a vendor and provided information to the purchasing office, but we wanted to be sure you are aware of our company and our unique (offering, method, etc." Later you can mention your certification(s).
Skip to Common Actions Table (page 202)		

Marketing to Local Government

Situation	Action	Notes
The municipality or county requires certification?	Be sure that you have the proper certification. Some municipalities and counties have their own certification.	Some do not require a certification but instead use the "self-certifying" methods. This means that you declare you are 51-percent woman owned and they accept that declaration.
Lists of vendors are maintained by the purchasing department, but departments and individuals may also keep their own lists.	Complete the vendor registration form for the municipality or county. Be sure to accurately note your woman-owned status.	Many municipalities and counties maintain a list of vendors and keep information on file, but do not have an official vendor registration form. Normally they prefer that you send them a letter asking to be registered as a vendor include: > Business name and contact information stated in the body of the letter (not just on the letterhead). > Very brief description of the business. > List of products and/or services you want the opportunity to bid or propose. This is vital, they do not usually make assumptions. If they do they might not be accurate. > WOB certification information (or statement that you are a WOB if you are not certified).

Situation	Action	Notes
Most purchasing is done by the purchasing department.	Contact the purchasing staff and provide them information on your business and certifications. They normally want you to get to know you.	Purchasing offices are rule keepers, they: > Ensure purchased product or service is of proper quality and reasonably priced. > Ensure vendors are capable and financially sound. > Ensure that all vendors have an equal opportunity. > Ensure that the municipality/county procurement code is followed.
The municipality or county has staff assigned to work with woman- and minority-owned businesses?	Contact all appropriate staff and provide them information on your business.	Sometimes these folks will instruct you to complete the vendor registration form before they will talk with you. That is why this process directs you to complete the form *before* making contact.
You realize that the purchasing staff are not the users.	Contact the users (departments, offices, individuals) of your products or services and tell them about your business and certification(s).	Most purchasing departments/offices encourage vendors to contact the users of their product. Often a department, office, or individual will provide a list of vendors to notify when they submit a purchase request. If they do not know you, you will not be on the list.
Skip to Common Actions Table (page 202)		

Marketing to Public K-12 Education

Situation	Action	Notes
The school district requires certification?	Be sure that you have the proper certification.	Most school districts accept the certification from its home county or state. The district may also accept other certifications.
Lists of vendors are maintained by the purchasing department, but schools, departments, and individuals may also keep their own lists.	Complete the vendor registration form. Be sure to accurately note your woman-owned status.	Many school districts maintain a list of vendors and keep information on file, but do not have an official vendor registration form. Normally these folks prefer that you send them a letter asking to be registered as a vendor. This letter should include: > Business name and contact information stated in the body of the letter (not just on the letterhead). > Very brief description of the business. > List of products and/or services you want the opportunity to bid or propose to them. This is vital, they do not usually make assumptions; even if they do they might not be accurate. > WOB certification information (or statement that you are a WOB if you are not certified).

Situation	Action	Notes
The district has staff assigned to work with woman- and minority-owned businesses?	Contact all appropriate staff and provide them information on your business.	Sometimes these folks will instruct you to complete the vendor registration form before they will talk with you. That is why this process directs you to complete the form *before* making contact.
Most purchasing is done by the purchasing staff.	Contact the purchasing/procurement staff and provide them information on your business and certifications. They normally want to get to know you.	Purchasing/procurement offices are rule keepers, they: > Ensure the purchased product or service is of proper quality and reasonably priced. > Ensure vendors are capable and financially sound. > Ensure that all vendors have an equal opportunity. > Ensure that the district's purchasing rules are followed.

Situation	Action	Notes
You realize that the purchasing staff are not the users.	After receiving permission from the purchasing department, contact the users of your products or services and tell them about your business and certification(s).	Most school districts do not like for vendors to contact schools directly. The purchasing department/staff is charged with keeping things uniform and using the buying leverage of all the schools to obtain lower pricing (quantity discounts). They usually are okay with a vendor contacting district wide departments such as facility maintenance. It is very important to discuss any contacts with purchasing prior to making the contact. This does not necessarily apply to fund raising activities and products; purchasing does not usually get involved with these.
Skip to Common Actions Table (page 202)		

Marketing to Private Education

Situation	Action	Notes
The private education institution requires certification?	Be sure that you have the proper certification.	
Lists of vendors are probably maintained by the purchasing staff, but not always in as formal a method as public education institutions. Departments, campuses, and individuals may also keep their own lists. They may or may not have a vendor registration form.	If the institution has a vendor registration form, complete it. If they do not have a form, send a letter asking to be on their vendor list. Be sure to note your woman-owned status.	The letter should include: >Business name and contact information. >Very brief description of the business. >List of products and/or services you want the opportunity to bid or propose to them. This is vital, they do not usually make assumptions; even if they do they might not be accurate. >WOB certification information (or statement that you are a WOB if you are not certified). >References from other education institutions.
The institution has staff assigned to work with woman and minority-owned businesses?	Contact all appropriate staff and provide them information on your business.	

Situation	Action	Notes
Most of the purchasing is done by the purchasing department.	Contact the purchasing staff and provide them information on your business and certifications.	Private education institutions are not governed by any rules or goals for the use of woman- and minority-owned businesses. They, of course, cannot discriminate, but otherwise set their own policies and goals.
You realize that the purchasing staff are not the users.	Contact the users of your products or services and tell them about your business and certification(s).	Because these institutions set their own policies, you will need to be familiar with them so you do not overstep an important boundary. The normal protocol is to let the purchasing staff know that you will be making contact with other staff and faculty.
Skip to Common Actions Table		

Marketing to Business

Situation	Action	Notes
The business requires certification.	Be sure that you have the proper certification.	More details are provided in Chapter 11.
The business requires registration on a vendor list?	Complete the vendor registration form (follow the instructions precisely). Be sure to accurately note your woman-owned status.	There may be separate vendor lists for various divisions, projects or locations. It is important that you do your identification and qualifying research in order to determine which prospects are best for you.
The business catalogs and forwards information on woman, minority, or disadvantaged businesses to division, project, and location purchasers and users?	Provide the appropriate office/staff with information on your business including your certifications.	Purchasing staffers are rule keepers, they: > Ensure purchased product or service is of proper quality and reasonably priced. > Ensure vendors are capable and financially sound. > Ensure that all vendors have an equal opportunity. > Ensure that any special requirements or set asides for the use of woman, minority, or disadvantaged businesses are enforced.

Situation	Action	Notes
The business has staff assigned to helping them reach their goals for the use of woman-owned businesses?	Contact all appropriate staff and provide them information on your business.	Usually these folks prefer that you complete the vendor registration form before they talk with you. This person(s) is normally charged with identifying, and sometimes qualifying, woman, minority, and disadvantaged businesses.
You realize that the purchasing staff are not the users.	Contact the users of your products or services and tell them about your business and certification.	Begin the conversation or correspondence with a phrase such as this: "We have already registered as a vendor and provided information to the purchasing office and XX (small bus liaison, supplier diversity director or whatever is appropriate), but we also want to make you aware of our unique ..."
In your research you found that there might be subcontracting opportunities with this particular business.	Contact the appropriate person (that is, subcontracting manager, project manager) to find out the procedure for registering as a potential subcontractor. Some businesses have special application forms for potential subcontractors. Follow the procedure precisely. Be sure to accurately make note of your woman-owned status and certifications.	Smaller businesses may not have procedures or forms, but you should still provide your information in writing. A letter with brochures is probably sufficient as long as you supply enough information for them to understand your capabilities and contact you.
Skip to Common Actions Table		

Common Actions

Situation	Action	Notes
You understand that you will need to remind the purchasing staff and users that you exist.	Establish a schedule for recontacting and following up. You should make contact at least every six months, more often if you think they may have an opportunity occurring before the six-month period is up. It is best to have a reason for recontact. Here are some suggestions: > You have a new product or service > You open a new location > You have a major change in your business > You receive a new certification > You have a new customer/client (preferably one that the prospect can relate to). > You can also contact them at holidays—not just Christmas/Hanukah, but maybe 4th of July, first day of spring, Halloween, etc. Another opportunity for contacting them is when they have a change, win an award, get a contract or grant, and so on.	If you do not establish the schedule you will probably not do the recontact and follow up that you should to keep your business in the minds of the purchasers and users.

Situation	Action	Notes
A prospect makes a request (information, credential, and so on).	You fulfill the request promptly and thoroughly. Be sure that the materials provided include a statement about your certification(s). Follow up to be sure they received your response and see if they need anything else.	One of the main complaints from purchasers is that vendors do not respond to requests. A secondary complaint is that the response is either not timely, complete, or professional.
You understand that purchasers and users are people.	Pay attention to them personally and respond appropriately. If they have a preference of procedure, format, or method then honor that. Thank them when they provide you time, information or guidance.	Keep in mind that they may have a preconceived attitude or prejudice about women business owners. No matter whether it is positive or negative you need to be aware of it and either capitalize on it or neutralize it as appropriate.
The prospect sponsors or participates in a trade fair, matchmaking event, or something similar.	You participate. Be sure to include information on your certification(s) in your materials.	Organizations (such as SBA) and government entities often sponsor reverse trade fairs where the agencies, departments, offices, and prime contractors have the booths and the vendors can visit and get information on doing business with them. The participants are looking for you and need WOBs to meet their goals. More information on participating in trade fairs and matchmaking events is provided later in this chapter.

Situation	Action	Notes
Some of your target prospects look for vendors and subcontractors on special registration Websites.	Find out which sites your targets use and register. Some sites charge so you need to evaluate them for value.	Some examples are: > Websites used by general contractors to find Subcontractors. > Websites used by insurance adjusters to find auto repair shops, fire, and water damage restoration, temporary housing, and so on. > Websites that are used by government entities.

General Advice

There are some broad pieces of advice that apply generally to using the woman-owned angle in marketing and selling. If you use these and the advice and guidelines in this book you will truly set yourself apart from your competitors.

Be Wise About Using the Woman-Owned Angle

You must know when and how to use the fact that you are a woman-owned business. If the prospect needs your business in order to meet a goal or get a contract, then you may want to lead with it. Sometimes being woman-owned adds to your value; you are qualified and capable to provide the needed product/service, but being woman-owned gives you an edge in a competitive situation. In this case you provide your woman-owned status as one of your credentials, verbally, and/or in printed materials. However, you probably do not want to lead with the fact that you are a woman-owned business. Consider using a sentence such as "In addition to X we can help you attain your supplier diversity goals." Sometimes it is best not to even mention that you are a WOB. Conditions that make this advisable include:

❐ Preconceived ideas about capability—try another angle, maybe focus on experience.

❐ Prospect has had a bad experience with W/MBEs—you cannot capitalize on a negative.

❐ It makes you appear to have a sense of entitlement. ("I should get your business because my business is woman owned.")

❐ Another angle works better.

❐ It does not matter.

❐ It is obvious and that's enough.

Learning about your prospects is the way to determine the best use, or non-use, of your woman-owned status. Without research you are guessing and guessing is risky.

Be Professional

All of your marketing materials and efforts need to be done in a professional manner. If purchasers do not know you or your business, they have little on which to judge you. Therefore one of the measurements they use is their impression of your professionalism.

Small, woman- and minority-owned businesses are sometimes tempted to scrimp on marketing materials. Unfortunately prospects may see you as too small if you do not have professional looking materials—note that I said professional, not expensive. Following are some recommendations on how to enhance their impression of you through marketing materials and ensure that they get the message that you are a woman-owned business.

❑ Use business cards and be sure to include contact information. Accurate contact information is far more important than a catchy phrase or unusual art. Include your WOB certification(s).

❑ Use stationery for your correspondence and bids. You can have some printed or you can use one of the many publishing software packages. You do not have to have a logo, but you do need to include the following:

- Business name
- Address
- Phone number
- E-mail address
- Website
- Certification (Because this information may not always be necessary, you may want to have a version with and one without)

❑ Use brochures because they give you an opportunity to provide concise information that demonstrates your competency. This is another place a publishing software package can help you. You can also use a marketing or advertising firm to develop and print them. Either way you should consider having a basic brochure shell with general information and space to add specific, tailored information for the various types of prospects—government, education, and business. The general information should include your certification(s).

❏ Establish a Website that has real information about your business (including your certifications). There are companies that provide templates that you can use to create your own Website; they will host it for you for as little as $10 a month. Or you can use a Website developer to build your site. Most business, government, and education entities do the majority of their business online. They want to see proof that you can also do business online and having a Website is considered the obligatory first step. One of the most important assets you gain from having a Website is that you get an e-mail address with the name of your business in it; this is more effective than having your e-mail address include your business name and the name of your Internet provider (that is, yourname@yourbusinessname.com is better than yourbusinessname@wellknowninternetprovider.com). Remember to include your certification or at least the fact that you are woman owned on the first page.

❏ Be sure that all your materials are consistent in information and look. Consistency stimulates confidence. If you cannot spend the money it takes to have a public relations/advertising firm do brand development, be sure you choose the same colors, fonts, clip art, and so on, so that your materials are not only professional but also recognizable. The consistent information should include your certifications.

❏ Be sure your materials are accurate. If you change anything—address, phone number, e-mail address, and so on—make sure you change it on your materials and Website. It does not do any good to put information out there if it is wrong.

Professional attitude and conduct will greatly differentiate you from your competition, even from other woman-owned businesses. Following are the common key indicators of professionalism as perceived by purchasers. This is sort of a "wish list" of purchasing staffers and users.

- ❒ Provide concise, printed information.
- ❒ Do not provide anything handwritten (except a thank you note).
- ❒ Respond promptly and thoroughly when a request is made.
- ❒ Never ignore a request, even if you have to say "no" or "I can't."
- ❒ Provide references in materials.
- ❒ Understand a prospect's business—what they do and how they do it.
- ❒ Never feel or convey entitlement because you are a woman or minority.
- ❒ Keep all information up to date and accurate; this includes your marketing materials and every place that you have registered as a vendor. It is frustrating to identify a possible vendor and not be able to contact them because their registration information is wrong. Even if a prospect tracks you down (and it's unlikely they will do that), their impression of you has been tainted.

Sometimes prospects will expect more from a woman-owned business than from others. (As stated before, this book is not about fighting a cause, but is intended to help woman-owned businesses make the most of the current realities.) Because of this sometimes unbalanced expectation, you must ensure that your professionalism is clear and cannot be used as an excuse not to do business with you.

Be in the Right Place at the Right Time

In addition to direct contact with prospects, as outlined in the tables of this chapter, you also need to keep your business in front of them through other channels. Following are some ideas about how to accomplish this.

Participate in the same organizations as your prospects. Some examples:

❐ Professional—AGC (Association of General Contractors), Mortgage Bankers Association, AMA (American Medical Association)

❐ Government/Education—State School Board Association, State Municipal Association, State Purchasers Association

❐ Conventional—Chambers of Commerce, civic organizations, and so on.

❐ Specialized—industry specific within Chambers (that is, manufacturers group), purchasing professionals groups

❐ Organizations that support development of woman-owned, minority-owned, or small business. (Remember that membership/participation in this type of organization by a business, government, or education entity indicates that they are serious about supplier diversity)

❐ SBA (Small Business Administration) matchmaking—affairs that bring purchasers and vendors together

Here are some suggestions for methods of participation:

❐ Take part in trade shows and meetings—being an exhibitor is a good idea, but being a speaker is even better, especially if you and a member of the organization make a presentation on a common problem/need that your business re-solved. (Example: You and a school district fa-cility maintenance director make a presentation on how your product/service reduced the district's annual expenses.)

❏ Use matchmaking events to meet your pros-pects—be sure you have your certification cre-dentials with you and that you have done the qualifying research before the event. If the event provides one-on-one sessions, time is usually lim-ited to 15 minutes, sometimes 30 minutes, and you need to use it to sell your business, not find out about the prospect. If you can illustrate how your product/service and WOB certification can specifically benefit them, you will stand out from the other businesses they meet during the event.

❏ Join or monitor the appropriate organizations so you can identify the prospects most likely to ben-efit from your woman-owned status and so that you will know the major issues and needs of pros-pects. Most organizations have Websites that provide this information. The best sources are press releases, president's message, and meeting agendas.

❏ Be careful how you spend your money on mem-berships, exhibit booths, and sponsorships. Make sure you understand the benefits and outcomes. You should consider alternatives, for example:

■ Instead of being a sponsor for a con-tinental breakfast at an organization's annual meeting, consider hosting a hospitality suite where you have their undivided attention as opposed to hoping the sign with your business name gets noticed.

- ■ Instead of paying for a membership, offer to teach a seminar in exchange for a membership. You not only save the cost of the membership, you also get in front of the group (be sure your materials are professional and include your certification information). Most organizations are always looking for speakers.

❑ Do not spend your money on a membership if you are not going to participate. Just being on the membership roster is not likely to bring you any business, no matter what the membership representative says.

❑ Always evaluate your participation and be sure that your actions and investment (money and time) sync with your woman-owned business marketing angle. This it not to say that you should not participate in something because the WOB angle is not suitable; just be sure you match the marketing angle with the audience.

Additional Tidbits

❑ There is no magic formula for marketing, no matter what angle you use. Marketing takes planning, effort, and persistence.

❑ People buy from people. Think about this: if you have used a company for a product or service in the past and know they also provide the new product or service for which you are now shopping, will you go first to that company or will you look in the phone book? Business, government, and education purchasers are likely to invite businesses they know to bid/propose before they will go to any vendor list. They must at least know your business exists if you are to get an opportunity.

☐ There is no shame in being a subcontractor instead of a prime contractor. Know your assets (being woman owned, for one), abilities, and limitations and make the most of them.

☐ Develop a marketing plan with a time schedule and stick to it; otherwise, something will always take precedence over marketing.

GLOSSARY

8(a)—A certification and developmental program for Small Disadvantaged Businesses from the Small Business Administration (SBA). This program includes financial and business counseling. Businesses must qualify as a disadvantage business and the owners must have a personal worth of less than $250,000. This certification provides some advantages in bidding opportunities on federal government projects.

Bid—The submission of a price or proposal to provide a specific product or service for a specific price.

CCR—Central Contractor Registration—the federal government's primary database of vendors. Vendors register with CCR, their information is validated and then shared with federal government purchasers. The database is also used by prime contractors on federal government projects.

Certification—Validation that a business or business owner meets specific qualifications. Most certifications for woman-owned businesses require that the business be 51-percent or more owned and managed by a woman or women. There are other requirements specific to individual certifications such as personal worth, geographical location, or social disadvantage.

DBE—Disadvantage business enterprise—a designation or certification that identifies a business as meeting specific criteria. Programs associated with DBE are designed to improve the opportunities for those receiving the designation. This term is used by some government entities and business as an all-inclusive designation instead having separate certifications for woman, minority, disabled, or veteran ownership. Federal and state departments of transportation use DBE.

DOT—Department of Transportation—can be federal or state.

FedBizOps—The federal government Website that provides postings of business opportunities with federal agencies. *www.fedbizopps.gov*

Goal—The target percentage or dollar amount that a government, education, or business entity will spend with woman- or minority-owned businesses.

HUB—Historically Underutilized Business—a term used by some businesses and government entities in place of minority or disadvantaged.

HUB Zone—A program by the Small Business Administration (SBA) to encourage economic development and produce jobs in specific urban and rural communities. Communities are designated as HUB Zones (HUB = Historically Underutilized Business).

MBE—Minority Business Enterprise—a business that is 51-percent or more owned and managed by a minority. Many times women are classified as a minority when it comes to business ownership.

Minority —This classification, as it relates to business ownership, is based on race or ethnicity and sometimes gender. It is dependent on the definition of the government, education, or business entity using the term.

OSDBU—Office of Small and Disadvantaged Business Utilization—This office is normally found in federal government agencies (each agency has one); however, some states may also use this term. The OSDBU is responsible for assisting its Agency in establishing and meeting its goals for the use of small and disadvantaged (woman, minority, and so on) businesses. It also is charged with assisting small and disadvantaged businesses in capitalizing on opportunities with its agency.

Prime Contractor—The business that has the contract with a government, education, or business entity, but uses other businesses as subcontractors to provide some of the products and/or services specified in the contract.

Procurement—A term used primarily by some government entities to identify the process of purchasing and obtaining products and services.

Procurement Code—The laws of a state, local government, or education entity that governs the purchasing and obtainment of products and services.

Prospect—A business, government, or education entity that a business has identified as a possible customer or client.

Purchase—Person at a prospect or client/customer that actually buys or contracts for products and services.

Purchasing—A term used to describe both the process of buying products and services and the department or office that does the buying.

RFP—Request for Proposal—The formal document that is used to solicit a proposal from vendors for specific products or services. An RFP is used when the associated project is complex and/or the buying entity wants the proposing vendors to do some design or provide suggestions. A RFP normally provide specific requirements and parameters, which the vendors are expected to strictly adhere to. Most government and education entities have rules that specify when they must use a RFP. Other related processes include: RFI (Request for Information) and RFQ (Request for Qualifications or Request for Quote).

SBA—Small Business Administration (*www.sba.gov*)—The federal agency established to strengthen the U.S. economy by providing aid, counseling, and assistance to small businesses. SBA makes available loan assistance, business improvement training, and counseling, certifications, and online resources for small and disadvantaged businesses. The agency provides a special Website for woman-owned business (*www.sba.gov/onlinewbc/*) and supplies funding for women's business centers throughout the United States. SBA also awards certifications [8 (a), SDB, HUB Zone] to disadvantaged businesses in order to qualify them for special opportunities with federal government agencies and prime contractors.

SBDC—Small Business Development Center(s)—A network of centers under the SBA that provides management assistance to start-ups and existing businesses. SBDCs are located throughout the United States and provide training and counseling services. Many SBDCs are associated with university systems.

SCORE—SCORE is an organization of volunteers that provide professional advice, counseling, and training for small businesses. This resource is primarily funded by the SBA. The organization is now simply called SCORE, but its name was originally an acronym that meant Service Corps of Retired Executives. Many of the volunteers are retired business professionals. *www.score.org*

SDB—Small Disadvantaged Business—A program from the small business administration (SBA) to assist socially disadvantaged businesses in having equal opportunity in obtaining business. The SBA provides a certification for businesses that qualify and whose owners have a personal worth of less than $750,000. The business owner must show that he/she is socially disadvantaged. This certification provides some advantages in bidding opportunities on federal government projects.

Set Aside—Federal government agencies, and sometimes state and local government entities, designate some opportunities as being available only to a specific type of business. The type may be 8 (a), SDB, woman-owned, minority-owned, small business, very small business, and so on. These designated opportunities are called "Set Asides."

Subcontractor—A business that contracts with the prime contractor on a government, education or business project to provide a portion of the products or services. The Subcontractor is responsible to and receives payment from the prime contractor. Many government and education projects require prime contractors to submit subcontracting plans stating goals for the use of small and woman/minority-owned businesses and possibly other business classifications.

Supplier Diversity—The practice of making a concerted effort to diversify the use of suppliers in order to be inclusive of all types of suppliers especially woman- and minority-owned businesses. One of the primary goals of supplier diversity is to promote equality for all suppliers and potential suppliers.

Supply Chain—The chain from raw materials to product or service consisting of suppliers, producers, distributors, retailers, service providers, recyclers, and many other functions. A simple supply chain illustration: A feed and seed store provides seeds and fertilizer to a farmer, the farmer grows corn and provides it to a local grocery store which sales it to consumers. The feed and seed store, the farmer and the grocery store are all links in the supply chain.

Tier I Supplier—In the supply chain a Tier I supplier is the first level of suppliers to a specific business; for instance a tire supplier is a Tier I supplier to an auto manufacturer. Many large businesses require their Tier I suppliers to have supplier diversity plans.

INDEX

ABOUT THE
AUTHOR

Janet W. Christy has spent the majority of her professional career in marketing, sales, and public relations positions. Today she uses that experience to help small, woman- and minority-owned businesses maximize and profit from their opportunities.

In 2003, Janet formed Leverage & Development, LLC, a consulting firm focused on helping small and woman/minority-owned businesses and government/education entities. The firm has several service offerings that assist businesses and governments in evaluating their assets and then developing plans to improve them and/or use them to accomplish specific goals.

Janet currently works with women- and minority-owned businesses to develop plans that will help them capitalize on being woman or minority owned. Her services include marketing research and planning, certification assistance, and sales guidance. She conducts workshops for woman- and minority-owned businesses through women's business organizations, chambers of commerce, colleges/universities, and economic development organizations. These workshops provide attendees with practical instruction, resources, and experience-based advice on such topics as: Should My Business Be Certified?; Capitalizing On Being Woman Owned; Guide to the Government Bidding Process; and Teaming, Partnering, and Subcontracting for Woman/Minority Owned Businesses.

Since early 2000, Janet has worked with several east coast municipalities and counties to determine strategies and develop plans for improving the entrepreneurial culture and services as part of their economic development efforts. She also works with municipalities and counties to develop small business incubators/resource centers and woman/minority business development Initiatives.

Janet has worked on both sides of the procurement process. Her experience includes both preparing RFPs (Request for Proposal) and RFIs (Request for Information) and responding to them. She currently works as a consultant for Small and woman/minority-owned businesses to aid them in responding to RFPs and bids. She also assists government and education entities in the development of RFPs and the evaluation of responses. She has aided several government and education entities successfully apply for grants related to entrepreneur development and support.

To contact Janet about speaking or conducting a workshop you can e-mail her at *janet@leverageanddevelopment.com* or call her at 864-244-4117. The Website for Leverage & Development, LLC is *www.leverageanddevelopment.com.*

This book can be ordered in bulk for your members or clients. Some quantity discounts may be available. For more information about ordering books visit the Career Press Website at *www.careerpress.com* or call 1-888-227-3371.